More of
AMERICA'S MOST
WANTED RECIPES

Also by Ron Douglas

America's Most Wanted Recipes

More of AMERICA'S MOST WANTED RECIPES

MORE THAN 200 SIMPLE AND DELICIOUS SECRET RESTAURANT RECIPES — ALL FOR $10 OR LESS!

RON DOUGLAS

ATRIA PAPERBACK

New York London Toronto Sydney

Several products displayed and mentioned in this book are trademarked. The companies that own these trademarks have not participated in, nor do they endorse, this book.

This book features a compilation of recipes and cooking tips based on personal interpretation of the foods listed. Through trial and error, each recipe was re-created to taste the same as, or similar to, its restaurant/brand counterpart, but they are not the actual recipes used by the manufacturer or creator.

The brand or restaurant names for the recipes have been included only as an aid in cataloging the recipes and do not imply authenticity or endorsement by the manufacturer or creator. All restaurant and company names are trademarks of their respective owners. Please see our Trademarks section at the end of this book for detailed trademark credits.

For the actual and authentic versions of the food products listed in this compilation, please patronize the individual restaurant or manufacturer.

ATRIA PAPERBACK
A Division of Simon & Schuster, Inc.
1230 Avenue of the Americas
New York, NY 10020

Copyright © 2010 by Verity Associates LLC

First Atria Paperback edition July 2010

ATRIA PAPERBACK and colophon are trademarks of Simon & Schuster, Inc.

For information about special discounts for bulk purchases,
please contact Simon & Schuster Special Sales at
1-866-506-1949 or business@simonandschuster.com.

The Simon & Schuster Speakers Bureau can bring authors
to your live event. For more information or to book an event,
contact the Simon & Schuster Speakers Bureau at
1-866-248-3049 or visit our website at www.simonspeakers.com.

Designed by Davina Mock-Maniscalco
Illustrations by Jason Snyder

Manufactured in the United States of America

10   9   8   7   6   5   4   3   2   1

Library of Congress Cataloging-in-Publication Data is available.

ISBN 978-1-4391-4826-6
ISBN 978-1-4391-5573-8 (ebook)

To Nia and Ryan

CONTENTS

INTRODUCTION

What an amazing journey it's been since the publication of *America's Most Wanted Recipes:*

From trying to create copycat restaurant recipes as a hobby to helping hundreds of thousands of foodies save money and have fun by making their favorite dishes at home.

From sharing a few recipes on my blog to cooking them live on national television.

From working with my wife to crack the codes on secret recipes to collaborating with professional chefs and a community of more than 225,000 members at RecipeSecrets.net.

From self-published ebook sold on the Internet to international best seller available wherever books are sold.

We have truly come a long way.

Over the years, we've received thousands of e-mails from happy customers who have made these recipes at home and shared them with their families. It gives us great pleasure to see our hard work bringing enjoyment to so many people.

In today's difficult economic environment, this cookbook is really a symbol of the times. It contains more than two hundred restaurant recipes that you can make at home for under $10 (assuming you already have the basics, like spices). Now you can save money and still enjoy your favorite foods for a fraction of their usual cost. But besides just the cost savings, there are many reasons you'll love *More of America's Most Wanted Recipes:*

- The fun reactions and the kudos you'll receive when guests try a dish you've made that tastes just like the restaurant's.
- The fact that you already know what the dish is supposed to taste like before it's made and that you can have fun comparing it with the restaurant version.

- Being able to customize these restaurant dishes to your own taste and dietary guidelines.
- The ability to enjoy copycat versions of dishes from several different restaurants in one setting. For example, a starter from T.G.I. Friday's, an entrée from Outback Steakhouse, and a dessert from The Cheesecake Factory can all be had during one meal.
- Adding variety to your home cooking by spicing up dinnertime with new dishes your family is sure to love.
- Improving your cooking by learning some of the special techniques that go into re-creating some of the most popular dishes in the world.

All of these benefits are now available to you at your fingertips!

If this cookbook helps put a smile on your face, then all the research, testing, tweaking, measuring, and trial and error we've gone through to deliver recipes that taste just like the restaurants' will have been well worth the effort.

A substantial collective effort has gone into creating copycat recipes that taste just like their restaurant counterparts. This cookbook is the result of the efforts of my wife and me, our community of taste testers at RecipeSecrets.net, and our team of expert recipe cloners. I would like to acknowledge a few key members of our team and briefly introduce them to you:

Chef Todd Mohr

Chef Todd is a graduate of Baltimore International College, School of Culinary Arts. After culinary school, he was an executive chef, taught a college culinary program, started and operated a successful catering company, and then finally opened The Cooking School in Cary, North Carolina, in 2007. Today Chef Todd actively teaches cooking online through his WebCookingClasses.com and also manages the "Cooking Class Blog" on RecipeSecrets.net.

Chef Tom Grossmann

Raised in New York City, Chef Tom was taught from a young age how to prepare family recipes. As a teenager, he worked in several restaurants, learning tips and techniques from great chefs. After high school, he obtained a degree in restaurant management. Today Chef Tom is an active cook, writer, and blog manager for "The Secret Recipe Blog" at Recipe Secrets.net.

Marygrace Wilfrom (aka Kitchen Witch)

Marygrace comes from a long line of professional cooks and has more than fifty years of cooking experience. She's been the head cook at several different restaurants, where her tasks have included teaching line cooks and prep cooks. She is affectionately known on the Internet as "Kitchen Witch" and can often be found on our Secret Recipe Forum helping home cooks with their cooking questions.

If you're new to *America's Most Wanted Recipes,* you're about to experience a cookbook like no other. If you're curious about your favorite restaurant recipes, you no longer have to wonder, "How did they make that?" The answers are here in this book.

There are more than two hundred recipes from fifty-six different restaurants in this cookbook. These recipes were handpicked on the basis of popularity and requests received from our subscribers at Recipe Secrets.net. They include our versions of restaurant favorites like:

Applebee's Deadly Chocolate Sin—page 13
Applebee's Santa Fe Chicken Salad—page 16
The Cheesecake Factory Chicken Madeira—page 53
The Cheesecake Factory Louisiana Chicken Pasta—page 55
Chili's Spicy Garlic-and-Lime Shrimp—page 72
Chipotle Mexican Grill Barbacoa Burritos—page 75
Famous Dave's Barbecue Sauce—page 95
Golden Corral Rolls—page 109
Hard Rock Cafe Blackened Chicken Penne Pasta—page 116
KFC Grilled Chicken—page 140
Olive Garden Tuscan Garlic Chicken—page 187
Outback Steakhouse Bloomin' Onion—page 189
P.F. Chang's China Bistro Orange Peel Chicken—page 221
Shoney's Country Fried Steak—page 261

T.G.I. Friday's Spicy Cajun Chicken Pasta—page 286
Uno Chicago Grill Classic Deep-Dish Pizza—page 295

Every recipe in *More of America's Most Wanted Recipes* has been tested and tweaked to taste just like the original. Although we can offer only "clones" of these famous dishes, we are confident that if you follow the instructions, you won't be able to tell the difference.

There are tips throughout the book in which I share my personal experience and suggestions for making these dishes, as well as tips for saving money, saving time, and preparing healthier alternatives.

I encourage you to make the most of this cookbook by trying these and many of the other recipes at RecipeSecrets.net yourself. I'm sure you'll discover some new family favorites that will be on the "most wanted" list in your kitchen.

Enjoy!

Ron Douglas

COST-CUTTING IDEAS

- Before you shop, take a tour through your pantry and your refrigerator. Be organized! Don't buy what's already hiding in your kitchen.
- If you're a fan of coupons, remember this: It's not what you save, it's what you spend. If you save thirty cents on something you wouldn't ordinarily buy anyway, you haven't really saved anything.
- A typical fruit item is significantly larger than one serving. Most people would be just as happy eating a small apple as eating a large one, so buy smaller fruits!
- Make simple meals. One-dish meals can contain your meat, your vegetable, and your bread.
- Learning simple kitchen tasks, such as how to cut up a chicken instead of buying boneless, skinless chicken breasts, will save you money.
- Eat before you shop. When it comes to shopping smart, hunger can affect spending, because when we're hungry, everything in the market looks good.
- Buy your meats from a butcher, preferably local, and *not* from a store that sells only prepackaged meat. Buying meat at a supermarket often leads people to buy more than they need, and it's often of a lower quality than meat bought from a local butcher. You can often get a much better price per pound than in the grocery store.
- Buy staples in bulk. Not only does this save on gas and driving time, but you will save money on your purchase—most of the time. A few things you can buy in larger sizes include flour, sugar, rice, and cheese.
- Buy in season. Everything costs less when it's in season and even less when it's local. The less distance the item has to travel, the less money has to be added to its base price. Fruits and vegetables also taste much better in season.

- Plan ahead and make a grocery list. Create a menu of what you want to eat for the whole week, and make a grocery list with all the missing ingredients plus whatever other items you ran out of during the previous week. Deciding what you want to eat once you are at the grocery store will not only cause you to buy more than you need and duplicate ingredients you already have at home, but you might often choose less healthy, more expensive foods.

TIME-SAVING IDEAS

Vegetables

- Buy prewashed salad greens in a bag. Buy prewashed and precut vegetables in salad packs. They cost a little more but will save you time.
- Keep prepared salad in a vacuum-seal plastic container for storage.
- Use a food processor to chop vegetables.
- Buy peeled and cut vegetables to save time.
- Keep frozen vegetables in your freezer—they are already prepared and easy to cook with.
- Prechop onions and other vegetables and keep in resealable plastic bags until ready to use. They will keep for about a week.

Meats

- Purchase boneless cuts of meat and thinly sliced meats—they cook much faster.
- You can buy already cut and marinated meats, particularly chicken, pork, and beef. These are available fresh for immediate cooking or frozen and can be kept in the freezer for a quick meal.
- Buy cooked rotisserie chicken. Available at every grocery store, it can be made into soup or broth, and the meat can be cut off and added to pasta or salads.
- If you like to save money by buying meat in bulk at large warehouse stores, this can be a time saver as well. Although you will need to spend the time cutting the meat into smaller portions at home, it can then be sealed with a vacuum sealer for airtight storage in your freezer. You can marinate the meat before freezing and even precook ground beef to have it ready for quick prep time later.
- Meatballs can be made and cooked in advance, then stored in your freezer. They can be added to sauces while cooking or microwaved and tossed on top of spaghetti.

Soups and Sauces

- Cook and freeze sauces and broths for quick use later. Soups freeze very well. Make several different types of soups and freeze them in small containers for quick lunches or dinners. Or pour your homemade broth into ice cube trays and freeze. Use the broth cubes to make quick pan sauces when sautéing meat.
- Marinara, bolognese, and puttanesca sauces freeze very well. Make ahead and keep them in the freezer for quick weeknight pasta dinners.

REFRIGERATOR AND FREEZER STORAGE CHART

Product	Refrigerator	Freezer
EGGS		
Fresh, in shell	4 to 5 weeks	Don't freeze
Raw yolks or whites	2 to 4 days	1 year
Hard cooked	1 week	Don't freeze well
Liquid pasteurized eggs or egg substitutes (opened)	3 days	Don't freeze
Mayonnaise	2 months	Don't freeze
DELI AND VACUUM-PACKED PRODUCTS		
Egg, chicken, tuna, ham, macaroni salads	3 to 5 days	Don't freeze well
Prestuffed pork and lamb chops, chicken breasts stuffed w/dressing	1 day	Don't freeze well
Store-cooked convenience meals	3 to 4 days	Don't freeze well
Commercial-brand vacuum-packed dinners with USDA seal (unopened)	2 weeks	Don't freeze well
GROUND MEAT AND STEW MEAT		
Ground beef and stew meat	1 to 2 days	3 to 4 months
Ground turkey, veal, pork, lamb	1 to 2 days	3 to 4 months
HAM AND CORNED BEEF		
Corned beef in pouch with pickling juices	5 to 7 days	Drained, 1 month

Product	Refrigerator	Freezer
HAM AND CORNED BEEF (*cont.*)		
Ham, canned, labeled "Keep Refrigerated"	6 to 9 months (unopened)	Don't freeze (unopened)
	3 to 5 days (opened)	1 to 2 months (opened)
Ham, fully cooked, whole	3 to 5 days	1 to 2 months
Ham, fully cooked, slices	3 to 4 days	1 to 2 months
HOT DOGS AND LUNCH MEATS	**(IN FREEZER WRAP)**	
Hot dogs	1 week (opened package)	1 to 2 months (opened package)
	2 weeks (unopened package)	1 to 2 months (unopened package)
Lunch meats	3 to 5 days (opened package)	1 to 2 months (opened package)
	2 weeks (unopened package)	1 to 2 months (unopened package)
FISH AND SHELLFISH		
Lean fish	1 to 2 days	6 months
Fatty fish	1 to 2 days	2 to 3 months
Cooked fish	3 to 4 days	4 to 6 months
Smoked fish	2 weeks	2 months
Fresh shrimp, scallops, crawfish, squid	1 to 2 days	3 to 6 months
SOUPS AND STEWS		
Vegetable- or meat-added or mixtures of both	3 to 4 days	2 to 3 months

Product	Refrigerator	Freezer
BACON AND SAUSAGE		
Bacon	7 days	1 month
Sausage, raw pork, beef, chicken, or turkey	1 to 2 days	1 to 2 months
Smoked breakfast links or patties	7 days	1 to 2 months
Summer sausage labeled "Keep Refrigerated"	3 months (unopened)	1 to 2 months (unopened)
	3 weeks (opened)	1 to 2 months (opened)
FRESH MEAT (BEEF, VEAL, LAMB, AND PORK)		
Steaks	3 to 5 days	6 to 12 months
Chops	3 to 5 days	4 to 6 months
Roasts	3 to 5 days	4 to 12 months
Variety meats (tongue, kidneys, liver, heart, chitterlings)	1 to 2 days	3 to 4 months
MEAT LEFTOVERS		
Cooked meat and meat dishes	3 to 4 days	2 to 3 months
Gravy and meat broth	1 to 2 days	2 to 3 months
FRESH POULTRY		
Chicken or turkey, whole	1 to 2 days	1 year
Chicken or turkey, parts	1 to 2 days	9 months
Giblets	1 to 2 days	3 to 4 months
POULTRY LEFTOVERS		
Fried chicken	3 to 4 days	4 months
Cooked poultry dishes	3 to 4 days	4 to 6 months
Pieces, plain	3 to 4 days	4 months
Pieces covered with broth or gravy	1 to 2 days	6 months
Chicken nuggets or patties	1 to 2 days	1 to 3 months

KITCHEN TIPS

- Use aluminum foil, parchment paper, or silicone liners on baking sheets and pans to save time on cleanup.
- Line your broiler pan with foil that can be thrown away when the food is done, leaving your pan clean.
- Spray the inside of your Crock-Pot with cooking spray. This helps prevent foods from sticking to the sides, and you will be surprised how much easier it is to clean the pot. Newer versions can be put in the dishwasher, too!
- Start with a clean kitchen and load the dishwasher as you cook—cleanup after the meal will be much easier.
- For cleaning smelly hands after chopping onions or garlic, just rub them on a stainless steel spoon. The steel will absorb the odor. Fresh coffee beans can also absorb nasty odors from your hands.
- If you happen to oversalt a pot of soup, just drop in a peeled potato. The potato will absorb the excess salt.
- When boiling eggs, add a pinch of salt to keep the shells from cracking.
- When storing empty airtight containers, throw in a pinch of salt to keep them smelling fresh.
- If you are making gravy and accidentally burn it, just pour it into a clean pan and continue cooking it. Add sugar a little at a time, tasting as you go to avoid oversugaring it. The sugar will cancel out the burned taste.
- Burned a pot of rice? Just place a piece of white bread on top of the rice for 5 to 10 minutes to draw out the burned flavor. Be careful not to scrape the burned pieces off the bottom of the pan when serving the rice.
- If you aren't sure how fresh your eggs are, place them in about 4 inches of water. Eggs that stay on the bottom are fresh. If only

one end tips up, the egg is less fresh and should be used soon. If it floats, it's past the fresh stage.

- Don't store your bananas in a bunch or in a fruit bowl with other fruits. Separate your bananas and place each in a different location. Bananas release gases that cause fruits (including other bananas) to ripen quickly. Separating them will keep them fresh longer.
- To keep potatoes from budding in the bag, put an apple in with them.
- If you manage to have some leftover wine at the end of the evening, freeze it in ice cube trays for easy addition to soups and sauces in the future.
- After boiling pasta or potatoes, let the water cool and use it to water your houseplants. The water contains nutrients that are great for plants.
- When defrosting meat from the freezer, pour some vinegar over it. Not only will it tenderize the meat but it will also bring down the temperature of the meat and cause it to thaw faster.
- The substance in onions that causes your eyes to water is located in the root cluster of the onion. Cut this part out in a cone shape, with the largest part of the cone around the exterior root section. Taking the outer layer off a peeled onion can also reduce the amount of eye-watering misery.
- Baking soda is an extremely effective cleaner. Use it with vinegar to deodorize drains and clean stovetops and sinks.
- If your salt is clumping up, put a few grains of rice in with it to absorb excess moisture.
- Keep iceberg lettuce fresh by wrapping it in a dry paper towel and storing it in a resealable plastic bag in the fridge.
- If your loaf of bread is starting to go stale, just put a piece of fresh celery in the bag and close it back up. For some reason, this restores a fresh taste and texture to the bread.
- Always keep an aloe vera plant in your kitchen. It's invaluable when you scrape your arm or burn your finger. Just break off a leaf and rub the gel from the inside on the injury.
- When making a soup, sauce, or casserole that ends up too fatty or

greasy, drop in an ice cube. The ice will attract the fat, which you can then scoop out.

- To reuse cooking oil without tasting whatever was cooked in the oil previously, cook a ¼-inch piece of ginger in the oil. It will remove any remaining flavors and odors.
- Water that has been boiled and allowed to cool will freeze faster than water from the tap. This comes in handy when you're having a party and need ice quickly.

Guide to Symbols in Recipes

Follow this key for helpful suggestions and fun facts.

SAVE MONEY
Watch your wallet without giving up restaurant-quality food with these tips on smart shopping and cost-effective preparation and storage.

SAVE TIME
These time-saving shortcuts will help you have dinner on the table in a fraction of the usual time.

HEALTHY CHOICE
Low-fat alternatives and waist-slimming suggestions make these dishes nutritious—and still delicious.

FOOD FOR THOUGHT
Test your culinary knowledge with these fun facts on rare ingredients and the art of cooking.

Secret Recipe Tip
Get the inside scoop and carefully guarded cooking tricks from top chefs across the country.

Restaurant History
Discover where it all began with these fascinating and fun accounts of how America's favorite restaurants rose to the top.

More of
AMERICA'S MOST
WANTED RECIPES

A&W

coney dog

Coney Island Chili Dog Sauce
1 pound ground chuck
1 teaspoon salt
¼ teaspoon pepper
One 6-ounce can tomato paste
1 cup water
1 tablespoon sugar
1 tablespoon yellow mustard
1 tablespoon onion flakes
2 teaspoons chili powder
1 teaspoon Worcestershire sauce
½ teaspoon celery seeds
¾ teaspoon ground cumin

Coney Dog
One 2-ounce Sabrett beef
  frankfurter (7½ inches long)
1 regular hot dog bun

Garnish (optional)
1 tablespoon chopped onion
1½ teaspoons shredded Cheddar
  cheese

1. Do ahead: Make the chili dog sauce. Sauté the ground chuck in a dry saucepan, crumbling it as it browns. Add the remaining sauce ingredients. Let the mixture simmer, stirring occasionally, until it thickens, 30 to 40 minutes. Let cool and refrigerate in a covered container until ready to use. Gently reheat 3 tablespoons, the portion needed for 1 serving.

2. Boil water in a saucepan and add the frankfurter; cover the pan, remove it from the heat, and let the hot dog sit for 10 minutes.

3. Microwave the bun for 10 seconds, remove the frankfurter from the water with tongs, and put it in the bun. Pour the warm chili sauce over the hot dog and garnish with the onion and cheese, if desired. Keep the napkins handy!

Note: The sauce freezes well and can be saved in small covered containers so you can reheat only what you need.

AT-HOME COST: $5

The A&W chain has been around since 1919, starting with frosty mugs of root beer and eventually becoming a full-service, nationally recognized restaurant.

A&W

hamburger

IT DOESN'T GET ANY BETTER THAN THIS 100 PERCENT USDA ALL-BEEF PATTY WITH KETCHUP, MUSTARD, AND PICKLES—ALL ON A TOASTED BUN WITH YOUR OWN "SECRET SAUCE."

3½ ounces ground chuck
2 teaspoons ketchup
1 teaspoon yellow mustard
Salt and pepper

1 jumbo hamburger bun, split in
half
2 Vlasic Ovals Hamburger Dill
Chips

1. Do ahead: Make the burger. Form the ground chuck into a patty that is 5 inches round and ½ inch thick. Place on a piece of waxed paper, cover with another piece, and freeze for 1 hour before cooking.

2. Do ahead: Make the secret sauce by combining the ketchup and mustard. Set aside.

3. Preheat the grill or broiler.

4. Place the partially frozen patty on the grill and cook for 2 to 3 minutes per side, until cooked through, seasoning both sides with salt and pepper.

5. Grill the split hamburger bun until toasted. Place the cooked burger on the bottom half, and top with the pickles. Spread the secret sauce on the top half of the bun and cover the burger.

6. Wrap the sandwich in a 12 by 12-inch sheet of foil and warm in a 250°F oven for 2 to 3 minutes, or wrap in plastic and microwave for 10 seconds.

Serves 1

AT-HOME COST: $3

A&W

original bacon cheeseburger

GO ALL OUT FOR THIS TRADITIONAL FAVORITE, WITH CRISP BACON, AMERICAN CHEESE, AND A TANGY SECRET SAUCE PILED ON 100 PERCENT USDA BEEF AND NESTLED IN A TOASTED SESAME SEED BUN.

3½ ounces ground chuck
2 teaspoons Kraft mayonnaise
2 teaspoons Kraft Original
  Barbecue Sauce
Salt and pepper
2 Oscar Mayer ready-to-serve
  bacon slices

1 jumbo sesame seed hamburger
  bun, split in half
1 thin slice tomato
1 slice American cheese
¼ cup chopped iceberg lettuce
2 Vlasic Ovals Hamburger Dill
  Chips

1. Do ahead: Make the burger. Form the ground chuck into a patty that is 5 inches round and ½ inch thick. Place on a piece of waxed paper, cover with another piece, and freeze for 1 hour before cooking.

2. Do ahead: Make the secret sauce by combining the mayonnaise and barbecue sauce. Set aside.

3. Preheat an electric grill or light a charcoal grill.

4. Place the partially frozen patty on the grill and cook for 2 to 3 minutes per side, until cooked through, seasoning both sides with salt and pepper.

5. Microwave the bacon for 30 to 45 seconds, until crisp. Drain on paper towels.

6. Grill the split hamburger bun until toasted. Place the cooked burger on the bottom half, and top with the tomato, bacon, cheese, lettuce, and pickles. Spread the secret sauce on the top half of the bun and cover the burger.

7. Wrap the sandwich in a 12 by 12-inch sheet of foil and warm in a 250°F oven for 2 to 3 minutes, or wrap in plastic and microwave for 10 seconds.

AT-HOME COST: $6

To make a double bacon cheeseburger, double the ground chuck and add an extra slice of American cheese between the 2 cooked patties. And if you're really up for it, add 2 more slices of crispy bacon to top the whole thing off!

A&W

papa burger

A DELICIOUS TASTE YOU WON'T FORGET—THE ALL-AMERICAN CHEESEBURGER PLUS A&W'S SIGNATURE TEEN SAUCE. ON A TOASTED SESAME SEED BUN, IT'S AN INSTANT HIT.

3½ ounces ground chuck
1 tablespoon Kraft mayonnaise
2 teaspoons hamburger relish
Salt and pepper
1 jumbo sesame seed hamburger bun, split in half

1 slice American cheese
¼ cup chopped iceberg lettuce
2 Vlasic Ovals Hamburger Dill Chips

1. Do ahead: Make the burger. Form the ground chuck into a patty that is 5 inches round and ½ inch thick. Place on a piece of waxed paper, cover with another piece, and freeze for 1 hour before cooking.

2. Do ahead: Make the Teen sauce by combining the mayonnaise and relish. Set aside.

3. Preheat an electric grill or light a charcoal grill.

4. Place the partially frozen patty on the grill and cook for 2 to 3 minutes per side, until cooked through, seasoning both sides with salt and pepper.

5. Grill the split hamburger bun until toasted. Place the cooked burger on the bottom half, and top with the cheese, lettuce, and pickles. Spread the Teen sauce on the top half of the bun and cover the burger.

6. Wrap the sandwich in a 12 by 12-inch sheet of foil and warm in a 250°F oven for 2 to 3 minutes, or wrap in plastic and microwave for 10 seconds.

Serves 1

AT-HOME COST: $4.75

To make a Super Papa Burger, double the amount of ground chuck and make 2 cooked burger patties, prepared as directed above, and put the cheese in between the cooked patties.

APPLEBEE'S
bourbon street steak

A JUICY, TENDER STEAK WITH THE ZING OF CAJUN SPICES, TOPPED WITH
SAUTÉED MUSHROOMS AND ONION.

½ cup steak sauce
¼ cup bourbon
2 teaspoons Cajun seasoning,
  plus extra as needed
1 tablespoon honey

2 teaspoons yellow mustard
Four 10-ounce beef rib steaks,
  round steaks, or chuck steaks
Sautéed mushrooms and onion,
  for steak topping

1. Make a marinade by mixing the steak sauce, bourbon, the 2 teaspoons Cajun seasoning, the honey, and mustard. A.1. is the usual favorite for steak sauce, and you can use whiskey or brandy in place of the bourbon if you prefer. Put the steaks in a resealable plastic bag with the marinade and give them a quick massage, making sure the marinade is evenly distributed. Let the steaks sit for at least 4 hours in the fridge (marinating overnight will enhance the flavors and tenderize the meat).

2. When you are ready to cook the steaks, preheat the broiler or light a charcoal grill. Line the broiler pan with foil or put a drip pan under the grill grate to catch the juices.

3. Remove the steaks from the marinade and drain them well. Season both sides of the meat with Cajun seasoning and discard the marinade. Broil or grill at medium-high heat until the steaks are lightly charred on one side, then turn them over and finish cooking. Remove the steaks to a warmed platter and let them sit for 2 to 3 minutes. Be sure to save any juices that collect on the platter to pour over the steaks.

4. Serve your steaks topped with the sautéed mushrooms and onion, plus any reserved juices from the steak platter.

Serves 4

AT-HOME COST: $9.25

Applebee's was founded in Atlanta, Georgia, by Bill and T.J. Palmer. They envisioned a restaurant that would provide full, quality service, consistently good food, and reasonable prices in a neighborhood setting. Their first restaurant, T.J. Applebee's Rx for Edibles & Elixirs, opened in November 1980.

APPLEBEE'S
club house grill

A TURKEY, HAM, CHEESE, AND TOMATO SANDWICH GRILLED TO PERFECTION ON THICK-SLICED FRENCH BREAD AND SERVED WITH A SIDE OF BARBECUE SAUCE.

1 tablespoon butter, softened
2 thick slices French bread
2 teaspoons mayonnaise
⅓ cup shredded Cheddar cheese
2 slices deli turkey

2 slices deli ham
2 slices tomato
2 teaspoons barbecue sauce, plus extra for dipping

1. Heat a griddle or skillet. Butter one side of each slice of French bread and grill the bread, buttered side down. While the bread is toasting, spread the top side of one of the slices of bread with the mayonnaise and half the Cheddar cheese.

2. Heat the turkey and ham in a microwave for about 10 seconds to warm them. First layer the turkey and tomato over the melting cheese and then spread with the 2 teaspoons barbecue sauce. Then continue with the ham and the rest of the Cheddar.

3. Cover with the other slice of grilled bread and slice on the diagonal. For an extra-toasty sandwich, turn it over one more time and put a salad plate on top to make sure the cheese on the inside melts and the bread is crunchy. Serve with extra barbecue sauce for dipping.

Serves 1

AT-HOME COST: $4

APPLEBEE'S
crispy orange chicken bowl

DELICATELY SEASONED BREADED CHICKEN COVERED IN A SPICY-SWEET ORANGE
GLAZE AND SERVED OVER ALMOND-RICE PILAF AND A TASTY MIX OF MUSH-
ROOMS, BROCCOLI, RED BELL PEPPER, SUGAR SNAP PEAS, AND SHREDDED CAR-
ROTS. TOPPED WITH TOASTED ALMONDS AND CRISPY NOODLES.

Orange Glaze

¼ teaspoon minced garlic
1 tablespoon vegetable oil
¼ cup slivered almonds
1 cup orange juice
½ cup packed light brown sugar
3 tablespoons orange marmalade
2 tablespoons soy sauce
½ teaspoon parsley flakes
¼ teaspoon red pepper flakes
Pinch of dried thyme
1 tablespoon rice wine vinegar

Almond-Rice Pilaf

3 tablespoons butter
¼ cup diced onion
¼ cup diced celery
1 cup converted rice
2¼ cups chicken broth
Pinch of salt
1 teaspoon parsley flakes
¼ cup slivered almonds, plus extra
  for garnish

Vegetables

1½ cups broccoli florets
1 cup sliced red bell pepper
¾ cup sugar snap or snow peas
¼ cup shredded carrot
1 cup sliced mushrooms (optional)

Chicken

1 egg, beaten
½ teaspoon salt
¼ teaspoon black pepper
1 tablespoon vegetable oil, plus
  extra for frying
2 pounds boneless, skinless chicken
  breasts, cut into 2-inch pieces
½ cup plus 1 tablespoon cornstarch
¼ cup all-purpose flour

Topping

½ cup crispy chow mein noodles

1. Do ahead: To make the orange glaze, lightly sauté the minced garlic in
   the vegetable oil—don't let the garlic burn, or it will taste bitter. Add
   all the remaining ingredients and bring the mixture to a boil; then

reduce the heat and simmer until the sauce has thickened to a glaze consistency, 12 to 15 minutes. It can be reheated if necessary.

2. Do ahead: Make the almond-rice pilaf. Heat the butter and lightly sauté the onion and celery until tender, but not browned. Add the rice and stir until all the grains are coated with the butter and have turned opaque. Add the chicken broth, salt, and parsley flakes and bring to a boil, then cover tightly and reduce the heat to low. Cook the rice until all the broth has been absorbed, 12 to 15 minutes. Stir in the almonds while fluffing the pilaf with a fork (using a spoon will mash the grains and make the pilaf gummy). The rice can be reheated if necessary.

3. Steam the vegetables in a steamer basket on the stovetop or in a microwave. To save some time, you can use a bag of frozen Asian-style vegetables, available at the supermarket.

4. To make the chicken: Whisk the egg with the salt, black pepper, and the 1 tablespoon vegetable oil and add the chicken pieces. In a separate bowl, combine the cornstarch and flour, mixing well. Add the chicken pieces a couple at a time and coat them thoroughly with the cornstarch mixture, then set them side by side on a baking sheet. Finish the whole batch this way. Fry the coated chicken pieces in vegetable oil until they are a light golden brown, 3 to 4 minutes—do not overcook, or the chicken will be tough. Remove the pieces with a slotted spoon to drain on paper towels.

5. To serve, toss the chicken and vegetables in the orange glaze and serve over a bed of almond-rice pilaf, topped with the crispy noodles and garnished with slivered almonds.

Serves 4 to 6

AT-HOME COST: $8.50

APPLEBEE'S
deadly chocolate sin

A DECADENT CHOCOLATE CAKE DRIZZLED WITH RASPBERRY COULIS.

Raspberry Coulis
One 10-ounce package frozen raspberries in heavy syrup, thawed

Cake
½ pound (2 sticks) plus 2 tablespoons unsalted butter, softened
6 ounces semisweet chocolate
2 ounces unsweetened chocolate
1 teaspoon vanilla extract
4 eggs, at room temperature, beaten
4 egg yolks, at room temperature, beaten

½ cup packed light brown sugar
6 tablespoons cornstarch

Garnish
1 pint fresh raspberries
12 sprigs fresh mint
or
12 triangular cookies
12 chocolate pieces

Special Equipment
Twelve 4-ounce ovenproof ramekins
Double boiler

1. Do ahead: Make the raspberry coulis. Process the thawed berries in a blender and strain through a fine-mesh strainer to remove the seeds. Refrigerate until needed.

2. Preheat the oven to 275°F. Butter the bottom and sides of each ramekin with the 2 tablespoons butter and set the ramekins aside on a baking sheet.

3. In the top of a double boiler, place the semisweet and unsweetened chocolates, the ½ pound butter, and the vanilla extract. Set over simmering water and stir until melted. Keep the heat low so the butter and chocolate melt slowly—if the pot is too hot, the butter will separate into oil and the chocolate will taste burned.

4. In a large mixing bowl, combine the eggs, egg yolks, and brown sugar. Beat at high speed until thickened and increased in volume, 5 to 7 minutes. Reduce the speed to low and slowly incorporate the cornstarch,

1 tablespoon at a time; then turn the mixer back up to high and continue to beat until soft peaks form, about 5 minutes.

5. Using a rubber spatula, gently fold the chocolate mixture into the beaten eggs until well blended. Spoon the mixture into each of the prepared ramekins and bake for 10 minutes, or until a toothpick inserted in the centers comes out clean. Let cool, cover with plastic wrap, and refrigerate until ready to serve.

6. To serve: Dip a dinner knife into hot water and run it around the sides of each ramekin. Invert the ramekin onto a serving dish, gently remove the ramekin from the plate, and spoon the raspberry coulis around the cake. Garnish each serving with the fresh raspberries and a mint sprig, or a cookie and a chocolate piece if you prefer.

Serves 12

AT-HOME COST: $6.50

APPLEBEE'S
mudslide

KAHLÚA, VANILLA ICE CREAM, AND CHOCOLATE SYRUP BLENDED TOGETHER AND TOPPED OFF WITH WHIPPED CREAM!

2 cups vanilla ice cream

2 ounces Kahlúa coffee liqueur

1 tablespoon chocolate syrup

Whipped cream

1. Combine the ice cream and the Kahlúa in a blender and process until smooth.

2. Swirl the chocolate syrup in a 16-ounce wineglass, holding the glass by the stem, until the sides of the glass are well coated. Pour the ice cream mixture into the glass and top with whipped cream. Add a straw (or maybe a spoon!) and enjoy.

Serves 1

AT-HOME COST: $4

APPLEBEE'S
santa fe chicken salad

GRILLED MARINATED CHICKEN BREAST ON A BED OF GREENS, GARNISHED WITH CRUSHED TORTILLA CHIPS, CHEDDAR CHEESE, AND GREEN ONIONS, WITH MEXI-RANCH DRESSING ON THE SIDE. SERVED WITH GUACAMOLE, SOUR CREAM, AND FRESHLY MADE PICO DE GALLO.

Pico de Gallo
3 large tomatoes, diced
1 large onion, diced
2 tablespoons diced jalapeño pepper
2 teaspoons salt
½ teaspoon black pepper
½ teaspoon garlic powder
½ cup chopped fresh cilantro
1 tablespoon olive oil
1 tablespoon white vinegar

Chicken
1 boneless, skinless chicken breast

Chicken Marinade
2 tablespoons gold tequila
¼ cup lime juice
2 tablespoons orange juice
¾ teaspoon minced jalapeño pepper
¾ teaspoon minced garlic
¼ teaspoon salt
¼ teaspoon black pepper
1 teaspoon fajita seasoning mix

Mexi-Ranch Dressing
¼ cup mayonnaise
¼ cup sour cream
1 tablespoon milk
2 teaspoons minced tomato
½ teaspoon white vinegar
1 teaspoon minced jalapeño pepper
1 teaspoon minced onion
¼ teaspoon dried parsley
¼ teaspoon Tabasco sauce
Pinch of salt
Pinch of dried dill
Pinch of paprika
Pinch of cayenne pepper
Pinch of ground cumin
Pinch of chili powder
Pinch of garlic powder
Pinch of black pepper

Mixed salad greens

Garnish
Shredded Cheddar cheese
Chopped green onions
Crushed tortilla chips

Sour cream, for serving
Guacamole, for serving

1. Do ahead: Make the pico de gallo by combining all the ingredients and refrigerating overnight in a tightly covered container.

2. Do ahead: Marinate the chicken by combining all the marinade ingredients (except the fajita seasoning mix) and refrigerating overnight in a tightly covered container, turning the chicken occasionally.

3. Do ahead: Make the dressing by thoroughly combining all the ingredients and refrigerating in a tightly covered container.

4. When it's time to prepare the salad, light a charcoal grill or preheat the broiler.

5. Remove the chicken from the marinade and shake off the excess. Season both sides of the chicken with the reserved fajita seasoning mix and grill the chicken until cooked through.

6. Prepare a bowl of your favorite mixed greens. Slice the chicken breast into short strips and place on top of the greens. Garnish the top of the salad with shredded Cheddar, green onions, and crushed tortilla chips. Serve with ramekins of pico de gallo, sour cream, and guacamole, as well as plenty of the Mexi-ranch dressing on the side.

Serves 1

AT-HOME COST: $5.90

You can also use a heavy, ridged cast-iron pan made for stovetop grilling—this type of pan is especially useful when you are grilling for one, as it saves you from having to light the grill.

AUNT CHILADA'S
sonoran enchiladas

HANDMADE ENCHILADAS, DEEP-FRIED AND TOPPED WITH ENCHILADA SAUCE AND CHEESE.

2½ pounds masa harina
¾ cup shredded Cheddar cheese, plus extra for garnish
¼ cup diced onion

1½ teaspoons salt
All-purpose flour, for dusting
Vegetable oil, for deep-frying
2 cups enchilada sauce

1. In a large bowl, combine the masa harina, the ¾ cup cheese, the onion, the salt, and ¾ cup water. This will be a sticky mixture, so you might want to use the paddle attachment of a stand mixer.

2. Put a little flour on your hands and scoop up enough masa to make a ball the size of a tennis ball. On a floured board, pat the ball to an even thickness, about the size of a small salad plate. You can use a rolling pin for this step, but don't make the enchilada too big. Continue in this manner until all the masa has been used up. You should have 10 enchiladas.

3. Heat 3 inches of vegetable oil to 365°F in a small, deep skillet and fry the enchiladas, one at a time, until golden brown and puffy on both sides. Drain on paper towels.

4. Heat the enchilada sauce and pour over each enchilada. Serve garnished with the extra cheese.

Serves 4

AT-HOME COST: $6

Any extra enchiladas can be covered tightly in plastic wrap and frozen for later use.

Masa harina is corn flour and can be found with the other flours in the supermarket.

Originally a depot and general store, this historic Phoenix, Arizona, landmark dates back to the 1890s. Today, Aunt Chilada's not only carries on the century-old tradition of heartfelt southwestern hospitality, but also serves the finest Mexican food this side of the border.

BAHAMA BREEZE

roasted cuban bread with garlic-herb butter and tomato marinade

A WHOLE LOAF OF BREAD TOASTED WITH GARLIC-HERB BUTTER AND COVERED WITH VINE-RIPENED TOMATOES, PARMESAN CHEESE, AND FRESH CILANTRO AND BASIL.

Marinade for Tomatoes

½ cup white wine vinegar

¼ cup orange juice

¼ cup extra virgin olive oil

1 tablespoon lemon juice

1 tablespoon light brown sugar

1 tablespoon Dijon mustard

1 tablespoon minced garlic

1 teaspoon chopped fresh oregano

1 teaspoon chopped fresh parsley

¼ teaspoon salt

¼ teaspoon pepper

2 large tomatoes, sliced ¼ inch thick

Garlic-Herb Butter

4 tablespoons (½ stick) butter, softened

2 tablespoons extra virgin olive oil

1 tablespoon chopped green onion

½ teaspoon minced fresh thyme

1 teaspoon minced garlic

Roasted Cuban Bread

One 12-ounce loaf Cuban bread

¼ cup grated Parmesan cheese

3 tablespoons minced fresh cilantro, for garnish

¼ cup julienned fresh basil, for garnish

1. Do ahead: Combine all the marinade ingredients in a blender and process until smooth. Refrigerate in a tightly covered container until ready to use. One hour before serving, pour the marinade over the sliced tomatoes in a bowl and set aside.

2. Do ahead: Combine all the ingredients for the garlic-herb butter and mash with a fork to make sure everything is well blended. Refrigerate in a tightly covered container. Let it sit out for an hour or two to soften before using.

3. Light a charcoal grill or preheat the oven to 450°F. Center a rack in the middle of the oven.

4. Cut the bread in half lengthwise and spread the garlic-herb butter over both of the cut surfaces. Place, cut side down, on the grill, or lay cut side up on a baking sheet. Grill the bread for 3 to 4 minutes, or bake in the oven until lightly toasted.

5. Arrange the marinated tomatoes in an overlapping style down the length of each of the halves of bread, sprinkle with the Parmesan cheese, and grill or bake until the cheese is melted.

6. Slice each half into 8 portions and garnish with the chopped cilantro and basil. Serve warm.

Serves 6 to 8

AT-HOME COST: $6.50

Use a thick loaf of French or Italian bread if you can't find the Cuban bread.

Cuban bread is very similar to French and Italian bread. It's usually baked with a split down the middle and is noted for its crispy crust.

Bahama Breeze is an American restaurant specializing in Caribbean-inspired fresh seafood, chicken, and steaks. Founded in Orlando, Florida, in 1996, there are more than two dozen locations throughout the United States. Bahama Breeze is owned by Darden Restaurants, which is the largest full-service restaurant company in the world. Darden also owns Red Lobster, Olive Garden, and Longhorn Steakhouse.

BAHAMA BREEZE
seafood paella

ASSORTED SEAFOOD, CHICKEN, SAUSAGE, AND PEAS WITH YELLOW RICE.

8 ounces chicken tenders, cut into quarters

8 ounces jumbo shrimp, peeled and deveined

8 ounces jumbo sea scallops

8 ounces fresh fish, cut into 1-inch cubes

4 teaspoons Creole seasoning

2 tablespoons extra virgin olive oil

1 cup chicken broth

2 ounces chorizo, diced

6 mussels, debearded and scrubbed

¼ cup green peas

4 cups cooked yellow rice

Fresh cilantro sprigs, for garnish

1. Season the chicken, shrimp, scallops, and fish separately with the Creole seasoning, using 1 teaspoon for each.

2. Heat the oil in a skillet large enough to hold all the ingredients. Start with the chicken, sautéing until partially cooked through, then add the scallops, the fish, and the shrimp. Sauté for a few minutes, until the seafood is nearly cooked through.

3. Add the chicken broth, chorizo, and mussels. Simmer until the mussels open, and discard any that do not open.

4. Last, add the green peas and yellow rice, stirring frequently to make sure all the ingredients are evenly mixed. Serve garnished with fresh cilantro sprigs.

Serves 2 or 3

AT-HOME COST: $10

Yellow rice can be found in the rice sections of markets. It is usually a long-grain rice. Popular in the Mediterranean, it is colored with saffron and turmeric. Follow the package directions for preparation.

Chorizo is a Spanish sausage made from pork and seasoned with chiles, pepper, and paprika. It is also found in Latin American and Portuguese recipes.

BENIHANA

rocky's choice

SIRLOIN STEAK AND CHICKEN BREAST, TEPPANYAKI STYLE, WITH BENIHANA'S FAMOUS GINGER SAUCE AND CREAM SAUCE. A BOWL OF HOT STEAMED RICE MAKES AN EXCELLENT ACCOMPANIMENT TO THIS DINNER.

Ginger Sauce
1 cup sliced onion
¼ cup sliced peeled fresh
   ginger
Juice and chopped flesh of
   1 lemon
2 cups soy sauce
1 cup white vinegar

Cream Sauce
2 cups soy sauce
⅓ cup sesame paste (tahini)
1 cup heavy cream
Pinch of garlic powder
1 teaspoon dry mustard, dissolved
   in 1 teaspoon water

Steak
5 ounces sirloin steak, cut into
   bite-size pieces
½ clove garlic, crushed
Salt and pepper
1 teaspoon soybean oil
2 mushrooms, sliced into 8 pieces

Chicken
3 ounces boneless, skinless chicken
   breast, cubed
½ teaspoon soybean oil
1 mushroom, sliced into 4 pieces
1 tablespoon white wine
½ teaspoon sesame seeds
1 lemon, sliced

1. Do ahead: Combine all the ginger sauce ingredients in a blender and process until smooth. Set aside until needed.

2. Do ahead: Whisk together all the cream sauce ingredients and refrigerate in a covered container until ready to use.

3. Heat a large skillet. Rub the sirloin steak pieces with the garlic and season with salt and pepper. Add the soybean oil to the pan and sauté the steak pieces until they are cooked to your preferred doneness. Add the mushroom pieces and sauté quickly. Set the steak aside and keep warm.

4. In the same skillet, sauté the chicken pieces in the ½ teaspoon soybean oil. Add the mushroom pieces and stir frequently. Add the white wine

and sesame seeds and sauté until the chicken is cooked through and no longer pink. Set the chicken aside on a plate and cover with the lemon slices—keep warm.

5. Gently warm the cream sauce and serve with the chicken and mushrooms. Serve the ginger sauce at room temperature with the steak.

Serves 1

AT-HOME COST: $9.50

Use shrimp or pork in place of the chicken. You can also use olive oil in place of the soybean oil, and another citrus fruit, such as an orange or a lime, in place of the lemon.

All sauces can be refrigerated for about 1 week in a covered container.

Benihana started out as a tiny four-table restaurant in New York City's theater district before becoming an international chain. Diners sit around large tables where chefs chop, slice, stir-fry, and grill as part of the teppanyaki-style entertainment.

BENIHANA

sesame chicken

BITE-SIZE PIECES OF CHICKEN AND MUSHROOMS IN A LIGHT LEMON-SOY SAUCE, SPRINKLED WITH SESAME SEEDS. SERVE WITH YOUR FAVORITE FRIED RICE.

1 teaspoon soybean oil
1 boneless, skinless chicken breast, cut into bite-size pieces
Salt and pepper
½ teaspoon lemon juice
1 teaspoon soy sauce
½ teaspoon sesame seeds
2 mushrooms, sliced into 8 pieces

1. Heat the oil in a skillet and sauté the chicken pieces, seasoning with salt and pepper. When the chicken is white and firm to the touch, add the lemon juice, soy sauce, and sesame seeds.

2. Add the mushroom pieces and sauté with the chicken for 2 to 3 minutes, until the chicken is cooked through.

Serves 1

AT-HOME COST: $3

BENIHANA

yakisoba dinner

JAPANESE STIR-FRIED NOODLES WITH CHICKEN AND VEGETABLES IN A SPECIAL SAUCE WITH SESAME SEEDS.

Yakisoba Sauce

2 tablespoons Worcestershire sauce

2 tablespoons ketchup

2 tablespoons soy sauce

2 tablespoons oyster sauce

Chicken and Noodles

2 boneless, skinless chicken breasts, diced

1 tablespoon cornstarch

2 tablespoons vegetable oil

1 carrot, cut into bite-size pieces

¼ head cabbage, cut into bite-size pieces

15 shiitake mushrooms, sliced

4 green onions, cut into thin strips

Three 4-ounce packages yakisoba noodles, cooked according to the package directions

8 ounces bean sprouts

Garnish

Ao nori (see Note)

Pickled ginger (*beni-shoga*)

1. Do ahead: Make the yakisoba sauce by combining all the ingredients. Refrigerate until needed.

2. Coat the chicken in the 1 tablespoon cornstarch. In a wok or large skillet, heat the oil and sauté the chicken for about 3 minutes, then add the vegetables and stir-fry until they are crispy-tender. Add the cooked soba noodles and stir-fry for about 1 minute.

3. Add ⅓ cup water and cover the wok or skillet to let the vegetables and noodles steam a little. Remove the lid and add the yakisoba sauce and continue to stir-fry a few minutes more.

4. Top with the bean sprouts and garnish with a few sprinkles of the *ao nori* and a few julienned slices of the pickled ginger.

Note: *Ao nori* is a Japanese seasoning/condiment of seaweed and sesame seeds.

AT-HOME COST: $6

Yakisoba noodles are made from wheat flour and are similar to ramen noodles. If you can't find either noodle, you might substitute spaghettini or other thin pasta made from whole wheat.

BRAVO! CUCINA ITALIANA

penne mediterranean

SPINACH, SUN-DRIED TOMATOES, PINE NUTS, OLIVE OIL, AND FETA CHEESE, TOSSED WITH MULTIGRAIN PASTA.

1 tablespoon dry-packed sun-dried tomato

1½ tablespoons olive oil

1 teaspoon chopped garlic

½ cup vegetable broth

2 tablespoons unsalted butter

2 tablespoons crumbled feta cheese

Salt and pepper

8 ounces multigrain penne, cooked according to the package directions

½ cup baby spinach

1 teaspoon pine nuts

1. Put the sun-dried tomato in some warm water for about 30 minutes to soften.

2. Heat the olive oil in a skillet and sauté the garlic and sun-dried tomato. Add the vegetable broth, butter, and 1 tablespoon of the feta cheese; stir to blend. Season with salt and pepper.

3. Add the cooked pasta and the spinach to the skillet, stirring to blend all the ingredients. Once the spinach begins to wilt, add the remaining 1 tablespoon feta and top with the pine nuts.

Serves 2

AT-HOME COST: $5

You can substitute regular or whole wheat penne for the multigrain. You may wish to slice the sun-dried tomato if it was packed whole. Save the water it was soaked in and add to the vegetable broth for a little extra flavor.

 Bravo! Cucina Italiana is a growing chain now in twenty states, serving fresh, made-to-order authentic Italian meals, prepared in full view of their guests.

BRAVO! CUCINA ITALIANA

pasta woozie

ALFREDO-STYLE FETTUCCINE WITH SAUTÉED SHRIMP AND FRESH SPINACH.

10 small shrimp, peeled and deveined

1 teaspoon chopped garlic

3 tablespoons olive oil

¾ cup Alfredo sauce, homemade or store-bought

1 tablespoon unsalted butter

8 ounces fettuccine, cooked according to the package directions

½ cup baby spinach

1. Sauté the shrimp and garlic in the olive oil. When the shrimp are cooked through, add the Alfredo sauce and butter.

2. Add the cooked fettuccine and toss with the sauce, then add the spinach at the last minute—the heat of the sauce will wilt it.

Serves 2

AT-HOME COST: $8.50

For a final garnish, sprinkle a little grated Parmesan cheese over the top.

For a variation, use sautéed chicken or Italian sausage in place of the shrimp.

BUCA DI BEPPO
chicken saltimbocca

JUICY SAUTÉED CHICKEN BREASTS, LAYERED WITH FRESH SAGE AND PRO-
SCIUTTO, AND TOPPED WITH ARTICHOKE HEARTS, CAPERS, AND A DELICATE
LEMON-BUTTER SAUCE.

Four 5-ounce boneless, skinless
   chicken breasts
¼ teaspoon salt
1 tablespoon minced fresh sage
4 slices prosciutto
½ cup all-purpose flour
2 tablespoons olive oil
½ cup white wine

¾ cup artichoke hearts,
   quartered
¼ cup lemon juice
1 tablespoon butter
¼ cup heavy cream
2 tablespoons drained capers,
   for garnish

1. Season the chicken breasts with the salt and sage. Lay a slice of prosciutto on each breast and pound it with a meat mallet until the breast is
   a little less than ½ inch thick. Lightly dredge with the flour.

2. Heat the oil in a skillet and sauté the chicken, prosciutto side down,
   until golden brown on both sides, turning once. Remove the chicken
   from the pan and discard the excess oil. Deglaze the pan with the white
   wine and add the artichoke hearts with the lemon juice, butter, and
   cream.

3. Let the mixture simmer until it begins to thicken. Taste for seasonings.
   To serve, pour the sauce over the chicken breasts and garnish with the
   capers.

Serves 4

AT-HOME COST: $8

Artichoke hearts come frozen, canned, or marinated. If using marinated ones, be sure to rinse off the marinade before adding them. Frozen artichokes should be thawed before using.

Prosciutto is an Italian dry-cured ham. It comes sliced paper thin and is often shredded as a topping or wrapped around melon and figs for a traditional Italian appetizer.

The first Buca di Beppo opened its doors in 1993 in the basement of a Minneapolis apartment building. Today, the chain has eighty-three locations nationwide, specializing in authentic, family-style Italian dining inspired by northern and southern Italian cuisine. In September 2008, Buca, Inc., was acquired by Planet Hollywood.

BUCA DI BEPPO

chicken with lemon

TENDER SAUTÉED CHICKEN BREASTS TOPPED WITH A DELICATE LEMON-BUTTER SAUCE AND CAPERS.

4 large lemons
Two 6-ounce boneless chicken
    breasts, skin on
Salt and pepper
1 cup all-purpose flour

¼ cup olive oil
¼ cup white wine or chicken broth
4 tablespoons (½ stick) unsalted
    butter, softened
Small handful of drained capers

1. Cut 3 of the lemons in half and squeeze the juice through a strainer and set it aside. Quarter the remaining lemon and save for garnish.

2. Season the chicken with salt and pepper and lightly dredge with the flour. Heat the oil in a skillet large enough to hold the 2 breasts, and sauté them, skin side down, until golden brown; then turn them over and sauté until cooked all the way through.

3. Add the white wine (or broth) and simmer until the liquid is reduced by half. Remove the cooked breasts to a warm plate and keep warm.

4. Take the pan off the heat and add the butter. Add the lemon juice as you quickly whisk the butter. The heat of the pan will be enough to melt the butter and emulsify it with the lemon juice.

5. Drizzle the lemon-butter sauce over the chicken breasts and garnish with the capers and the reserved lemon wedges.

Serves 2

AT-HOME COST: $4.50

Capers are the unopened flower buds from the caper bush—pickled and peppery.

BUCA DI BEPPO
chopped antipasto salad

A CLASSIC ITALIAN CHOPPED SALAD, FEATURING ITALIAN MEATS AND CHEESES, FRESH TOMATOES, RED ONION, CUCUMBERS, PEPERONCINI, AND ITALIAN VINAIGRETTE. A ZESTY TASTE OF ITALY IN EVERY BITE.

1½ cups iceberg lettuce, chopped
2 tablespoons pepperoni, diced
2 tablespoons mortadella, diced
2 tablespoons red onion, diced
2 tablespoons Provolone cheese, diced
¼ cup cucumbers, diced
2 tablespoons Gorgonzola cheese, crumbled
2 tablespoons feta cheese, crumbled

2 tablespoons peperoncini, chopped
½ teaspoon dried oregano
½ cup Italian vinaigrette dressing, homemade or store-bought

Garnish
¼ cup Roma tomatoes, diced
3 whole peperoncini
2 black olives
2 green olives

1. Toss all the salad ingredients with the dressing and mound on a single chilled plate, or separate onto two plates.
2. Garnish with the diced tomatoes, the peperoncini, and the olives.

Serves 1 as an entrée or 2 as a side salad

AT-HOME COST: $5.50

This salad can easily be adapted to your liking by adding or substituting ham, salami, or soppressata, or other Italian cheeses and cured meats.

An easy and healthy vinaigrette can be made from olive oil and lemon juice with fresh or dried basil.

Mortadella is an Italian cured pork sausage that is studded throughout with pork fat and delicately flavored with anise seeds and garlic. Peperoncini are small, mildly flavored peppers that are pickled whole.

BUCA DI BEPPO
bruschetta

HOT FROM THE OVEN, THIS BRUSCHETTA CAN BE SERVED WITH ANY MEAL, SOUP, OR SALAD.

Bruschetta Topping
1 pound Roma tomatoes
2 tablespoons fresh basil, finely
  chopped
¼ cup olive oil
1 clove garlic, minced
¾ cup red onion, diced
Salt and pepper

Bruschetta
Garlic, lightly smashed
1 loaf Italian or French bread,
  cut into 1-inch-thick slices
Olive oil

1. Cut the tomatoes in half and remove the seeds. Cut the tomatoes into ½-inch dice. Toss them with the remaining topping ingredients and leave at room temperature.

2. Preheat the oven to 400°F.

3. Rub smashed garlic over the bread slices and drizzle with olive oil. Place the slices on a baking sheet and lightly toast in the oven. Top with the bruschetta mixture and serve warm.

Serves 6 to 8

AT-HOME COST: $4.50

CALIFORNIA PIZZA KITCHEN

tuscan hummus

THEIR ORIGINAL RECIPE OF TUSCAN WHITE BEANS PUREED WITH SESAME, GAR-
LIC, LEMON, AND SPICES, GARNISHED WITH FRESH ROMA TOMATOES, BASIL,
AND GARLIC. SERVE WITH YOUR CHOICE OF WARM PLAIN OR HONEY-WHEAT
PITA BREAD.

Hummus
One 30-ounce can cannellini beans,
   rinsed and drained
10 cloves garlic, peeled
$\frac{1}{2}$ cup sesame paste (tahini)
$\frac{1}{4}$ cup lemon juice
$\frac{1}{4}$ cup olive oil
1 tablespoon plus $\frac{1}{2}$ teaspoon soy
   sauce
1 $\frac{1}{2}$ teaspoons salt
1 $\frac{1}{2}$ teaspoons ground cumin
Pinch of ground coriander
$\frac{1}{2}$ teaspoon cayenne pepper

6 pita breads, warmed

Garnish
2 tablespoons julienned fresh
   basil
Diced Roma tomatoes
Minced garlic

1. Combine the beans and garlic in a blender and process on low speed
    until the beans are coarsely ground. Add the sesame paste and increase
    the blender speed to puree.

2. Slowly add the lemon juice, olive oil, and soy sauce, then finish with the
    salt, cumin, coriander, and cayenne. If the mixture is too thick, add a
    little water with the blender running. Refrigerate in a covered container
    until ready to serve.

3. Preheat the oven to 250°F.

4. Place the pitas on a baking sheet and heat in the oven until they are
    warm. Garnish the hummus with the basil, tomatoes, and garlic. Cut the
    pitas into wedges and serve with the chilled hummus.

Serves 4 to 6

AT-HOME COST: $6.50

 Cannellini beans are similar to navy beans and Great Northern beans.

Hummus is a traditional Middle Eastern condiment popular in many Mediterranean countries. While this Tuscan hummus dish uses cannellini beans, the main ingredient in hummus has traditionally been chickpeas.

CARRABBA'S ITALIAN GRILL

chicken bryan

GRILLED CHICKEN BREAST TOPPED WITH GOAT CHEESE, AND A BASIL-LEMON-BUTTER SAUCE WITH SUN-DRIED TOMATOES.

Sun-Dried Tomato Sauce
1 tablespoon minced garlic
1 tablespoon minced onion
2 tablespoons butter
½ cup white wine
¼ cup lemon juice
1½ cups julienned oil-packed
  sun-dried tomatoes
¼ cup chopped fresh basil
½ teaspoon salt
½ teaspoon white pepper

10 tablespoons cold unsalted
  butter, cut into small pieces

Chicken
6 boneless, skinless chicken breasts
1 to 2 tablespoons extra virgin
  olive oil
½ teaspoon salt
½ teaspoon black pepper
8 ounces goat cheese, crumbled,
  at room temperature

1. To make the sun-dried tomato sauce, sauté the garlic and onion in the butter until soft. Add the white wine and lemon juice and simmer until reduced by half, 8 to 10 minutes. Stir in the sun-dried tomatoes, basil, salt, and white pepper, blending well. Set aside.

2. Light a charcoal grill to high heat.

3. Brush the chicken with the oil and season with the salt and black pepper. Grill, turning once, until the chicken is cooked through and no longer pink in the middle. Remove to a serving platter. Sprinkle the goat cheese evenly over the breasts and keep warm while you finish the tomato sauce.

4. Reheat the tomato sauce. Add the pieces of cold butter, one at a time, to the tomato sauce, whisking constantly. Pour the sauce over the chicken breasts and serve warm.

Serves 6

AT-HOME COST: $9.50

Carrabba's Italian Grill, founded in Houston in 1986, is not your typical restaurant chain. Its founders, Johnny Carrabba and Damian Mandola, both come from a long line of restaurant families.

CARRABBA'S ITALIAN GRILL

mussels in lemon-butter sauce

FRESH CANADIAN COVE MUSSELS FROM PRINCE EDWARD ISLAND STEAMED IN PERNOD AND LEMON JUICE.

Clarified Butter
4 tablespoons (½ stick) unsalted butter

Mussels
2 tablespoons extra virgin olive oil
2 pounds mussels, debearded and scrubbed
2 tablespoons chopped onion
2 tablespoons chopped garlic
2 tablespoons Pernod
Juice of ½ lemon
2 tablespoons julienned fresh basil

Lemon-Butter Sauce
2 tablespoons minced onion
2 tablespoons minced garlic
¼ cup plus 2 tablespoons lemon juice
2 tablespoons white wine
Salt and white pepper
2 tablespoons cold unsalted butter, cut into small pieces

1. Do ahead: Make the clarified butter by melting the 4 tablespoons butter over very low heat until the solids rise to the top. Carefully skim off the solids and strain the remaining liquid through a coffee filter placed in a strainer. Clarified butter can be refrigerated until ready to use. Store in a covered container and bring back to room temperature before using. You will use this butter to make the lemon-butter sauce.

2. In a large skillet, heat the olive oil. Add the mussels, cover with a lid, and steam for a few minutes. Add the onion, garlic, Pernod, and lemon juice. Cover once again for a few minutes, then add the basil. Discard any mussels that don't open. Remove from the heat and keep covered while you make the lemon-butter sauce.

3. Heat the clarified butter and lightly sauté the onion and garlic, just until soft. Add the lemon juice and white wine, then season to taste with salt and white pepper, simmering a couple of minutes to reduce the liquid.

Take the pan off the heat and whisk in the cold butter, piece by piece, until the sauce is emulsified.

4. Uncover the mussels and gently heat, adding the lemon-butter sauce and blending well.

. . . .

Serves 2

. . . .

AT-HOME COST: $8.50

Pernod is a licorice-flavored liqueur from France. You may want to substitute similarly flavored ouzo, sambuca, or anisette.

CARRABBA'S ITALIAN GRILL

pollo rosa maria

GRILLED CHICKEN BREASTS FILLED WITH FONTINA CHEESE AND PROSCIUTTO, TOPPED WITH MUSHROOMS AND A BASIL-LEMON-BUTTER SAUCE.

Clarified Butter
4 tablespoons (½ stick) unsalted butter

4 boneless, skinless chicken breasts, butterflied
4 slices prosciutto
¼ cup grated Fontina cheese
3 cloves garlic, minced
½ small onion, chopped

¼ cup white wine
1 cup sliced mushrooms
4 tablespoons (½ stick) cold unsalted butter, cut into small pieces
½ teaspoon salt
½ teaspoon white pepper
½ cup chopped fresh basil
Juice of 1 lemon

1. Do ahead: Make the clarified butter by melting the 4 tablespoons butter over very low heat until the solids rise to the top. Carefully skim off the solids and strain the remaining liquid through a coffee filter placed in a strainer. Clarified butter can be refrigerated until ready to use. Store in a covered container and bring back to room temperature before using. Use this butter to make the butter sauce.

2. Light a charcoal grill.

3. Cook the chicken breasts, turning once, until they are cooked through and no longer pink. Set aside until cool enough to handle.

4. Take 1 slice prosciutto and 1 tablespoon of the Fontina and cover one half of each cooked breast, then fold over and hold closed with a toothpick. Set aside and keep warm.

5. In a skillet, heat the clarified butter and sauté the garlic and onion until soft. Deglaze the pan with the white wine, then add the mushrooms and whisk in the 4 tablespoons cold butter. Season with the salt and white pepper and simmer until the mushrooms are just cooked

through. Add the basil and lemon juice. Pour over the warm chicken breasts and serve.

Serves 4

AT-HOME COST: $9

CARRABBA'S ITALIAN GRILL
rigatoni campagnolo

A LIGHT SAUCE OF ITALIAN SAUSAGE, TOMATOES, RED BELL PEPPER, AND ONION, TOSSED WITH RIGATONI, AND TOPPED WITH A SPRINKLE OF GOAT CHEESE.

¼ cup extra virgin olive oil
8 ounces bulk Italian sausage
½ cup minced onion
1 medium red bell pepper, julienned
2 cloves garlic, minced
¼ cup dry white wine
4 cups minced canned whole tomatoes, with juice
Pinch of red pepper flakes

Salt and black pepper
1 pound rigatoni pasta, cooked according to the package directions
2 tablespoons julienned fresh basil
¼ cup grated Pecorino Romano cheese
4 ounces Caprino or other goat cheese, crumbled

1. In a skillet, heat the oil and sauté the sausage, crumbling it as you stir, until cooked through and browned. Add the onion and bell pepper and sauté until tender. Add the garlic and cook for 1 minute more.

2. Add the wine and simmer for about 3 minutes. Add the tomatoes and their juice, the red pepper flakes, and salt and black pepper to taste.

3. Bring the mixture to a boil for 1 minute, then reduce the heat and simmer until the sauce has thickened. Stir in the cooked pasta and toss with the basil and Pecorino Romano. Simmer for a few minutes more and serve with a sprinkling of the goat cheese on top.

Serves 4

AT-HOME COST: $9

Substitute chèvre, French goat cheese, if you can't find Caprino.

Use turkey or chicken sausage in place of pork sausage.

CARRABBA'S ITALIAN GRILL
stuffed mushrooms parmigiana

TENDER MUSHROOMS STUFFED WITH ONION, GREEN BELL PEPPER, PEPPERONI, AND PARMESAN.

12 to 16 mushrooms, stems removed and reserved
2 tablespoons butter
1 medium onion, minced
2 ounces pepperoni, diced
¼ cup minced green bell pepper
1 small clove garlic, minced
About 12 Ritz crackers, finely crushed (enough to make ½ cup)

3 tablespoons grated Parmesan cheese
1 tablespoon chopped fresh parsley
½ teaspoon seasoned salt
Pinch of pepper
¼ teaspoon dried oregano
About ⅓ cup chicken broth

1. Preheat the oven to 325°F. Fill a shallow 13 by 9-inch baking dish with ¼ inch of water.

2. Mince the mushroom stems and sauté them in a skillet with the butter, onion, pepperoni, bell pepper, and garlic. Sauté over low heat until the vegetables are cooked through and most of the liquid has evaporated.

3. Add the crushed crackers, Parmesan, parsley, seasoned salt, pepper, and oregano, mixing well. Add as much of the broth as necessary to just moisten the mixture—the crackers should soak most of it up. Let the mixture cool enough to handle.

4. Fill the mushroom caps with the mixture and carefully place them in the baking dish. Bake for about 25 minutes, or until they are cooked through.

Serves 3 or 4

AT-HOME COST: $5

CARRABBA'S ITALIAN GRILL

tagliarini picchi pacchiu

FINE PASTA IN A SAUCE OF CRUSHED TOMATOES, GARLIC, OLIVE OIL, AND BASIL.

4 ounces angel hair pasta

2 large cloves garlic, sliced

4 Roma tomatoes, diced

¼ cup extra virgin olive oil

4 to 6 fresh basil leaves, coarsely chopped

Pinch of salt

Pinch of pepper

1. Cook the pasta according to the package directions.
2. Sauté the garlic and tomatoes in the olive oil until the garlic is soft. Add the basil and season with the salt and pepper. Toss with the cooked angel hair.

Serves 1

AT-HOME COST: $4.50

THE CHEESECAKE FACTORY

bang-bang chicken and shrimp

A SPICY THAI-FLAVORED VEGETABLE CURRY, WITH PEANUTS, CHILI OIL, AND COCONUT, SERVED OVER CHICKEN, SHRIMP, AND STEAMED WHITE RICE.

Curry Sauce
2 teaspoons chili oil
¼ cup minced onion
2 tablespoons minced garlic
2 teaspoons minced peeled fresh ginger
1 cup chicken broth
¼ teaspoon salt
¼ teaspoon pepper
½ teaspoon ground cumin
½ teaspoon ground coriander
½ teaspoon paprika
¼ teaspoon ground mace
¼ teaspoon ground turmeric
3 cups coconut milk

Vegetables
2 medium carrots, julienned
1 small zucchini, julienned
½ cup frozen peas

Peanut Sauce
¼ cup creamy peanut butter
4 teaspoons sugar

1 tablespoon soy sauce
1 teaspoon lime juice
1 teaspoon rice wine vinegar
½ teaspoon chili oil

Garnish
1½ cups flaked unsweetened coconut
½ teaspoon parsley flakes, crumbled
2 tablespoons chopped peanuts
2 green onions, julienned

Chicken and Shrimp
2 boneless, skinless chicken breasts, cut into bite-size pieces
16 large shrimp, peeled and deveined
¼ cup cornstarch
½ cup vegetable oil

4 cups cooked white rice

1. Do ahead: Make the curry sauce. Heat the chili oil in a large skillet over medium heat and add the onion, garlic, and ginger. Sauté until soft, then add the chicken broth, the salt and pepper and the spices; stir well

to combine all the ingredients. Simmer for about 5 minutes, then add the coconut milk and bring to a quick boil. Reduce the heat and simmer until the sauce thickens, about 20 minutes.

2. Do ahead: Very lightly steam or microwave the carrots, zucchini, and frozen peas, then drain and add to the curry sauce. Simmer until the vegetables are tender. Cover and refrigerate until ready to use. Gently reheat before using.

3. Do ahead: Make the peanut sauce. In a small saucepan over medium-low heat, combine the peanut butter, sugar, soy sauce, lime juice, rice wine vinegar, chili oil, and 2 tablespoons water. Stir to combine, then let the mixture come to a low simmer. Remove from the heat, cover the pan, and let cool. The mixture can be refrigerated until ready to use, but should be brought back to room temperature first and then gently reheated.

4. Do ahead: Toast the coconut in an oven preheated to 300°F. Spread the flakes on a baking sheet and toast carefully, stirring every 10 minutes, until lightly and evenly browned. Let cool completely before storing in a resealable plastic bag or covered container.

5. Coat the chicken and shrimp with the cornstarch. In a large skillet or wok, heat the oil and sauté the chicken first, until cooked almost all the way through, and then the shrimp, stir-fried until pink. Drain the chicken and shrimp on paper towels.

6. Divide the rice into 4 small bowls. Mound a bowl of the hot steamed rice onto each serving plate by inverting the bowl onto the center of the plate and then gently removing it. Spoon some of the chicken and shrimp around the rice on each plate and spoon some of the warm curry sauce over them, being careful not to get any on the rice.

7. Lightly spoon the peanut sauce over the dish, mostly on the rice, and garnish the rice with a pinch of the parsley, a bit of chopped peanuts, and a few of the julienned green onions. Finish with the toasted coconut sprinkled over the chicken and shrimp.

Serves 4

AT-HOME COST: $9

 The Cheesecake Factory was started by Evelyn Overton in 1949 as a small-scale bakery operated out of her family's basement in Detroit. Today it's a major chain and has much more on the menu than just cheesecake.

THE CHEESECAKE FACTORY
chicken madeira

THEIR MOST POPULAR CHICKEN DISH! SAUTÉED CHICKEN BREASTS WITH FRESH ASPARAGUS AND MELTED MOZZARELLA CHEESE, COVERED IN MUSHROOM MADEIRA SAUCE, AND SERVED WITH MASHED POTATOES.

8 asparagus spears
1 tablespoon olive oil
4 boneless, skinless chicken breasts, pounded ¼ inch thick
Salt and pepper

Madeira Sauce
2 tablespoons olive oil
2 cups sliced mushrooms

3 cups Madeira wine
2 cups beef broth
1 tablespoon butter
¼ teaspoon pepper
4 slices mozzarella cheese

Mashed potatoes, for serving

1. Do ahead: Cook the asparagus in salted boiling water for 3 to 5 minutes. Transfer to a bowl of ice water to stop the cooking. The asparagus should still be crisp-tender. Set aside and gently reheat when needed.

2. In a large skillet, heat the 1 tablespoon olive oil. Season the chicken breasts with salt and pepper and sauté for 4 to 6 minutes per side, until cooked through. Remove and keep warm.

3. In the same skillet, prepare the sauce: Add the 2 tablespoons olive oil and sauté the mushrooms for about 2 minutes; then add the Madeira, beef broth, butter, and pepper. Bring the mixture to a boil and lower the heat, simmering for about 20 minutes, or until the sauce has been reduced to one-quarter of its volume and is a rich dark brown. Keep the heat low so that the butter does not separate.

4. Preheat the broiler.

5. Put the chicken breasts in a baking pan and top each with a slice of mozzarella. Broil until the cheese begins to bubble and turns light brown. To serve, plate the chicken, place 2 asparagus spears on each

breast, and pour 3 to 4 tablespoons of the Madeira sauce over each breast. Serve with mashed potatoes.

Serves 4

AT-HOME COST: $9.50

Madeira is an aged wine from Portugal. For a substitute, try dry sherry or Marsala.

THE CHEESECAKE FACTORY
louisiana chicken pasta

PARMESAN-CRUSTED CHICKEN SERVED OVER BOW-TIE PASTA WITH MUSHROOMS, BELL PEPPERS, AND ONION IN A SPICY NEW ORLEANS SAUCE.

Cajun Sauce
1 small yellow bell pepper, chopped
1 small red bell pepper, chopped
¾ small red onion, chopped
3 cloves garlic, minced
1 teaspoon red pepper flakes
1 tablespoon butter
2½ cups heavy cream
1 cup low-salt chicken broth
¼ cup julienned fresh basil leaves
1 cup grated Parmesan cheese
1 cup sliced mushrooms
Salt and black pepper

Chicken
¾ cup bread crumbs
2 tablespoons all-purpose flour
¼ cup grated Parmesan cheese
1 cup milk
¼ cup vegetable or olive oil
6 boneless, skinless chicken breasts, pounded ¼ inch thick

Pasta
1 pound bow-tie pasta, cooked according to the package directions
Shaved Parmesan cheese, for garnish

1. Do ahead: Make the Cajun sauce by sautéing the yellow and red peppers, the onion, garlic, and red pepper flakes in the butter. Add the cream and chicken broth. Bring to a quick boil, then lower the heat and simmer until reduced by about one-quarter. Add the basil, Parmesan cheese, and mushrooms, then season with salt and black pepper. Simmer for a few minutes more, or until the mushrooms are cooked and all the ingredients are combined. Let cool, then set aside or refrigerate in a covered container; gently reheat the sauce when ready to use.

2. To prepare the chicken breasts, combine the bread crumbs, flour, and Parmesan cheese in a shallow bowl. Put the milk in a separate bowl. Heat the oil in a large skillet. Dip each breast in the bread crumb mixture,

then in the milk, and one more time in the crumbs, pressing gently to make sure the crumbs stick. Sauté until golden brown on both sides and cooked through (no longer pink in the middle). Keep each breast warm until all are done.

3. To serve, toss the cooked pasta with the Cajun sauce, ladle into individual bowls, and top with a chicken breast. Garnish with a little more Parmesan cheese on top.

Serves 6

AT-HOME COST: $9

THE CHEESECAKE FACTORY

pasta with mushroom bolognese

THIN SPAGHETTI TOSSED WITH MUSHROOMS, ONION, AND CARROT IN A RED
WINE—MARINARA SAUCE.

2 tablespoons carrot, cut into
small dice
2 tablespoons onion, cut into
small dice
4 ounces mushrooms, cut into
small dice (about 1 cup)
¼ cup olive oil
½ teaspoon salt
¼ teaspoon pepper
1 tablespoon minced garlic
1 teaspoon chopped fresh thyme

¼ cup Madeira
1¼ cups marinara sauce,
homemade or store-bought
2 tablespoons butter
6 ounces spaghettini pasta, cooked
according to the package
directions
¼ cup grated Parmesan cheese
2 teaspoons chopped fresh
parsley

1. Lightly sauté the carrot, onion, and mushrooms in the olive oil in a large
   saucepan until soft. Season with the salt and pepper and add the garlic
   and thyme, stirring gently to combine the ingredients.

2. Add the wine to the vegetables, let it simmer a bit, then add the marinara sauce. Simmer a few minutes more, until the alcohol is cooked off,
   then whisk in the butter.

3. Add the cooked pasta to the sauce. Add half the Parmesan cheese, tossing
   well to combine. Plate the pasta in a warmed bowl and garnish with the
   remaining Parmesan and the parsley. Serve immediately.

Serves 1

AT-HOME COST: $4.50

Spaghettini is thinner than spaghetti. Angel hair pasta, spaghetti, or even vermicelli can be substituted.

CHEVYS FRESH MEX

mesquite-grilled chicken quesadillas

MESQUITE-MARINATED CHICKEN WITH MELTED CHEESE BETWEEN GRILLED FLOUR TORTILLAS.

Mesquite Marinade
1 teaspoon mesquite-flavored
  liquid smoke
½ teaspoon salt
Pinch of black pepper

1 boneless, skinless chicken breast

Spicy Barbecue Sauce
½ cup Bull's-Eye Original BBQ
  Sauce
¼ teaspoon cayenne pepper
Pinch of chili powder

Nonstick cooking spray

Vegetable Filling
⅓ cup sliced red bell pepper
⅓ cup sliced green bell pepper
⅓ cup sliced onion

Two 12-inch flour tortillas
12 ounces Monterey Jack cheese,
  shredded
Salsa, for serving

1. Do ahead: Make the marinade by combining all the marinade ingredients with ½ cup water. Marinate the chicken for at least 1 hour in the refrigerator.

2. Do ahead: Make the barbecue sauce by combining all the barbecue sauce ingredients. Refrigerate, covered, until ready to use.

3. Do ahead: Spray a skillet with cooking spray and sauté the vegetables until they begin to brown. Set aside.

4. Light a charcoal grill or preheat the broiler.

5. Remove the chicken from the marinade and shake off the excess, so that it doesn't splatter on the grill. Discard the marinade. Grill the chicken, turning once, until it is cooked through and no longer pink in the middle. When it's cool enough to handle, cut into bite-size pieces.

6. Heat a cast-iron skillet or nonstick frying pan that's the same size as or a little larger than the tortillas. If you have one, a griddle works best. Place

1 tortilla in the hot skillet and sprinkle one-quarter of the cheese over half of the tortilla, top with half of the vegetables, then half of the chicken. Spread a generous amount of the barbecue sauce over the chicken, and finish with another one-quarter of the cheese. Fold the quesadilla in half and turn it over; cook until the cheese is melted throughout. Slice into 4 pieces and repeat with the second tortilla. Serve with salsa.

Serves 4 as an appetizer

AT-HOME COST: $8

Chevys Fresh Mex was founded in 1986 and is owned by Real Mex Restaurants, the largest full-service casual dining Mexican restaurant company in the United States, with nearly two hundred restaurants operating in more than a dozen states.

CHI-CHI'S
mexican chicken salad

A BLEND OF SHREDDED CHICKEN, CHOPPED EGGS, AND SALSA COMBINED WITH SOUR CREAM AND MAYONNAISE; SERVED ON A BED OF LETTUCE.

1 cup Chi-Chi's Salsa (page 63) or store-bought salsa
1 pound boneless, skinless chicken breasts, cooked and shredded
2 hard-cooked eggs, finely chopped
1/2 cup sour cream

1/4 cup mayonnaise
2 tablespoons minced onion
1 teaspoon grated lime zest
1/2 teaspoon chili powder
1/4 teaspoon ground cumin
Lettuce leaves, for plate liners

1. Drain the salsa well—whether it's Chi-Chi's or some other, too much liquid will make the salad watery.

2. Place the salsa and all the remaining ingredients except the lettuce leaves in a large bowl and stir well to combine. Line 4 serving plates with lettuce leaves and mound the chicken salad on top of each.

Serves 4

AT-HOME COST: $6

You may wish to substitute your own or another brand for Chi-Chi's Salsa. Just make sure it is very well drained before tossing with the other ingredients.

CHI-CHI'S

old west oven-fried chicken

MEATY CHICKEN THIGHS BAKED IN A CORNFLAKE CRUST AND FLAVORED WITH
TACO SAUCE AND SPICES.

1 egg, beaten	1 teaspoon dried oregano
2 cloves garlic, minced	Pinch of ground cloves
1 cup store-bought taco sauce	Red pepper flakes (optional)
2 cups crushed cornflakes	1½ pounds chicken thighs, skin on
2 teaspoons chili powder	6 tablespoons (¾ stick) butter,
2 teaspoons ground cumin	melted

1. Preheat the oven to 375°F and grease a shallow baking dish that's large enough to hold the chicken thighs in a single layer.

2. In a shallow bowl, whisk together the egg, garlic, and the taco sauce. Put the crushed cornflakes and the dry seasonings in a resealable plastic bag. (Add the red pepper flakes if you like a little more spice!)

3. Dip the thighs in the egg mixture, then shake them, one at a time, in the bag with the cornflakes. Place in the baking dish, skin side up, and drizzle with the melted butter. Bake for about 45 minutes, or until the chicken is golden brown and cooked all the way through—no pink meat and the juices run clear.

Serves 4

AT-HOME COST: $6

Try this recipe with chicken breasts, drumsticks, wings, or even pork chops.

CHI-CHI'S

salsa

A SALSA RECIPE THAT CAN BE USED FOR SALADS, TACOS, OR ANY DISH CALLING FOR SALSA.

One 14-ounce can stewed
tomatoes, diced, with juice
2 green onions, diced
½ teaspoon salt

½ teaspoon pepper
2 medium tomatoes, diced
Dash of Tabasco sauce

1. In a saucepan, combine the stewed tomatoes, green onions, salt, and pepper and boil hard for 1 minute, then remove from the heat. Put half of the mixture in a blender or food processor and process to a medium grind; the mix should not be pureed.

2. Transfer to a bowl and add the remaining tomato mixture, the diced tomatoes, and the Tabasco sauce. Let cool, then refrigerate in a covered container. The salsa will last for up to 3 weeks in the refrigerator.

Make 2 cups

AT-HOME COST: $2.50

You can make this salsa as spicy as you like by adding cayenne pepper, red pepper flakes, or additional Tabasco sauce.

CHI-CHI'S

san antonio chili

CHILI WITH A SOUTHWESTERN FLAIR, SERVED IN BAKED TORTILLA BOWLS AND
GARNISHED WITH SOUR CREAM, SALSA, AND SHREDDED CHEESE.

Nonstick cooking spray

Tortilla Bowls
Four 10-inch flour tortillas,
flavored or plain

Chili
8 ounces each lean ground beef
and pork (or 16 ounces all
beef)
1 large jalapeño pepper, minced
3 tablespoons chili powder
Two 14.5-ounce cans diced
tomatoes with garlic and onion,
with juice

Two 15-ounce cans red kidney
beans, drained and rinsed
One 8-ounce can tomato sauce
One 14.5-ounce can chicken or
beef broth

Shredded Cheddar cheese, for
garnish
Sour cream, for serving
Salsa, for serving

1. Preheat the oven to 325°F.

2. Use 4 ovenproof bowls inverted on 2 baking sheets. Spray the outside of
each bowl with cooking spray and drape with a flour tortilla. Spray the
tortillas well and bake in the hot oven for about 10 minutes, or until
crisp and lightly browned. Remove carefully from the oven and set to
cool on racks.

3. Heat a large skillet coated with cooking spray and sauté the ground beef
and pork, breaking the meat up with a spoon as it browns. Add the
minced jalapeño and chili powder and simmer for about 8 minutes.
Add the diced tomatoes, beans, tomato sauce, and broth. Bring the
mixture to a boil, then reduce the heat and simmer, partially covered,
for 30 minutes, or until thickened.

4. Put 1 tortilla shell on each plate and fill with the chili. Garnish with shredded cheese, and serve ramekins of sour cream and salsa on the side of the plate.

Serves 4

AT-HOME COST: $9.50

Substitute ground turkey or chicken for the beef-pork combination. Serve with fat-free cheese and fat-free sour cream.

CHILI'S
asian lettuce wraps

CRISP LETTUCE CUPS FILLED WITH ASIAN-FLAVORED STIR-FRIED CHICKEN, SERVED WITH TWO DIPPING SAUCES.

Stir-Fry Sauce
1 teaspoon cornstarch
1/3 cup soy sauce
1/4 cup sugar
1/4 cup rice wine vinegar
1 tablespoon Asian sesame oil
2 teaspoons sesame seeds
1 teaspoon red pepper flakes
1 teaspoon chili oil
1/2 teaspoon minced peeled fresh ginger

Sesame-Ginger Dipping Sauce
3/4 teaspoon cornstarch
1/4 cup sugar
1/4 cup rice wine vinegar
1/4 cup soy sauce
1 teaspoon minced peeled fresh ginger
1 teaspoon Asian sesame oil
1/2 teaspoon sesame seeds
1/4 teaspoon minced garlic
Pinch of red pepper flakes
Pinch of parsley flakes

Peanut Dipping Sauce
1/2 cup creamy peanut butter
1/2 cup water
2 tablespoons white vinegar
1/2 teaspoon minced peeled fresh ginger
Pinch of red pepper flakes
1/4 cup granulated sugar
1/4 teaspoon minced garlic
1/2 teaspoon chili oil
1/2 teaspoon peanut oil
1 tablespoon packed light brown sugar

Chicken
1 tablespoon vegetable oil
4 boneless, skinless chicken breasts, sliced into strips
1/4 cup minced water chestnuts
1/4 cup sliced almonds
3 green onions, chopped
4 to 6 large lettuce leaves

1. Do ahead: Make the stir-fry sauce. In a small saucepan, blend the cornstarch and 1/4 cup water. Add all the remaining stir-fry sauce ingredients and bring to a boil. Lower the heat and simmer until the sauce has thickened. Set aside, or let cool and then refrigerate in a covered container until ready to use. If chilled, heat gently before using.

2. Do ahead: Make the sesame-ginger dipping sauce. In a small saucepan, blend the cornstarch and ¼ cup water. Add all the remaining sesame-ginger dipping sauce ingredients and bring to a boil, then lower the heat and simmer until the sauce has thickened. Set aside, or let cool and then refrigerate in a covered container until ready to use. If chilled, heat gently before using.

3. Do ahead: Make the peanut dipping sauce. In a small saucepan, blend all the peanut dipping sauce ingredients and whisk over low heat until smooth. Set aside, or let cool and then refrigerate in a covered container until ready to use. If chilled, heat gently before using.

4. To cook the chicken, heat the oil in a wok or skillet and add the chicken; sauté until cooked through. Add the water chestnuts and almonds and ¼ cup of the stir-fry sauce. Simmer, stirring frequently, for a couple of minutes, then add the green onions.

5. Portion the chicken filling onto the lettuce leaves, fold the leaves over the filling to wrap, and serve with the sesame-ginger and peanut dipping sauces on the side.

Serves 4 to 6

AT-HOME COST: $6.50

CHILI'S
boneless buffalo wings

CRUNCHY CHICKEN BREAST PIECES WITH A SPICY HOT SAUCE AND A COOL BLUE CHEESE DRESSING.

1 cup all-purpose flour
2 teaspoons salt
½ teaspoon black pepper
¼ teaspoon cayenne pepper
¼ teaspoon paprika
1 egg, beaten
1 cup milk
2 boneless, skinless chicken breasts, each sliced into 6 pieces

4 to 6 cups vegetable oil
1 tablespoon butter or margarine
¼ cup Crystal or Frank's hot sauce

For Serving
Celery sticks
Blue cheese dressing, homemade or store-bought

1. In a medium bowl, combine the flour and dry seasonings and whisk until well blended. Separately, whisk together the egg and milk.

2. Dip each piece of chicken in the egg mixture, shake it a bit, then dip it in the flour mixture. Lay the pieces on a baking sheet and refrigerate for 15 minutes.

3. In a large skillet, heat 4 cups of vegetable oil to 375°F. Keep extra oil handy in case you need more to fry the chicken.

4. Melt the butter and add the hot sauce; set aside in a large bowl.

5. Fry the chicken pieces in batches, until golden brown and cooked through (no longer pink in the middle). Drain on paper towels. When all the chicken is cooked, put it in the butter–hot sauce mixture and toss. Serve with celery sticks and blue cheese dressing on the side.

Serves 2 as an entrée or 4 as an appetizer

AT-HOME COST: $8

For extra heat, add some cayenne pepper to the hot sauce mixture.

When the first Chili's restaurant opened in Dallas in 1975, the menu consisted of little more than burgers, chili, and tacos—yet there was a never-ending line out the door. Today, Chili's permanent and limited-time menu items are more exciting and innovative than ever.

CHILI'S
grilled caribbean salad

FRESH PINEAPPLE, MANDARIN ORANGES, DRIED CHERRIES, PICO DE GALLO, AND HONEY-LIME DRESSING. CHILI'S SERVES IT WITH YOUR CHOICE OF GRILLED CHICKEN, SHRIMP, OR BEEF.

Chicken
4 boneless, skinless chicken breasts
½ cup store-bought teriyaki marinade

Honey-Lime Dressing
¼ cup Grey Poupon Dijon mustard
¼ cup honey
1½ tablespoons sugar
1 teaspoon Asian sesame oil
1½ tablespoons apple cider vinegar
1½ teaspoons lime juice

Pico de Gallo
2 medium tomatoes, diced
½ cup diced onion
2 teaspoons diced jalapeño pepper
2 teaspoons minced fresh cilantro
Pinch of salt

4 cups chopped iceberg lettuce
4 cups chopped green leaf lettuce
1 cup chopped red cabbage
½ cup fresh pineapple, cut into chunks
½ cup mandarin orange slices
½ cup whole dried cherries
2 cups crushed tortilla chips

1. Do ahead: Marinate the chicken in the teriyaki marinade in a covered container for 2 hours in the refrigerator, turning occasionally.

2. Do ahead: In a small bowl, combine the honey-lime dressing ingredients, whisking well, and refrigerate in a covered container.

3. Do ahead: Combine the pico de gallo ingredients and refrigerate in a covered container.

4. Light a charcoal grill or preheat the broiler.

5. Remove the chicken from the marinade and shake off the excess. Cook each breast, turning once, 5 to 6 minutes per side, until cooked through and no longer pink in the middle. Set aside and keep warm.

6. Combine the lettuces with the cabbage and divide among 4 serving bowls. Top each salad with the pico de gallo, pineapple chunks, orange slices, cherries, and crushed tortilla chips.

7. Slice the cooked chicken into thin strips and divide among the salads. Serve with ramekins of honey-lime dressing on the side.

Serves 4

AT-HOME COST: $9.50

CHILI'S

spicy garlic-and-lime shrimp

SHRIMP WITH A HINT OF CITRUS DONE WITH A SOUTHWESTERN FLAIR.

Seasoning Mix
1 teaspoon salt
¼ teaspoon black pepper
¼ teaspoon cayenne pepper
¼ teaspoon parsley flakes
Pinch of garlic powder
¼ teaspoon paprika

Pinch of dried thyme
Pinch of onion powder

2 tablespoons butter
1 clove garlic, chopped
24 large shrimp, peeled and
   deveined
1 lime

1. Combine the seasoning mix ingredients and set aside.

2. Heat the butter in a skillet. Sauté the garlic for 10 seconds and add the shrimp. Squeeze the lime juice over the shrimp and sprinkle with the seasoning mix.

3. Sauté until the shrimp are pink and cooked through, 5 to 8 minutes.

Serves 4

AT-HOME COST: $8.50

The seasoning mix can be made ahead and stored in a covered container. You can also double or triple it and keep it on hand for other recipes.

CHIPOTLE MEXICAN GRILL
ancho chile marinade for meats

MARINATE YOUR CHOICE OF CHICKEN, BEEF, OR PORK FOR A TASTE OF THE SOUTHWEST.

Marinade
½ cup canned chipotles in adobo
4 cloves garlic
¾ cup white vinegar
½ medium onion, chopped
½ cup water
⅓ cup lime juice
4 teaspoons ground cumin

2 tablespoons paprika
1 teaspoon salt
½ teaspoon pepper

Chicken breasts, chicken thighs, sirloin steak, New York strip steak, or pork
Fresh cilantro sprigs, for garnish

1. Place all the marinade ingredients in a blender and process until smooth. Refrigerate in a tightly covered container.

2. Add your meat of choice and marinate in the refrigerator for 8 to 12 hours, turning occasionally.

3. Light a charcoal grill or preheat the broiler.

4. Drain the marinade from the meat and cook until done. Discard the marinade. Garnish the meat with fresh cilantro sprigs.

Makes about 2¼ cups, enough for 4 entrée servings

AT-HOME COST: $3

Shrimp and scallops can also be prepared with this marinade, but they must not stay in the sauce for over 30 minutes, as the acids will turn them opaque.

The first Chipotle Mexican Grill opened near the University of Denver in 1993. Chipotle's unique motto of "Food with Integrity" focuses on using ingredients that are unprocessed, family farmed, sustainable, nutritious, naturally raised, added-hormone free, organic, and artisanal.

CHIPOTLE MEXICAN GRILL
barbacoa burritos

BEEF BRAISED IN SPICY CHIPOTLE ADOBO AND WRAPPED IN A FLOUR TORTILLA
WITH YOUR CHOICE OF BEANS, RICE, OR VEGETABLES.

I dried guajillo pepper
½ teaspoon whole cumin seeds
¼ teaspoon whole cloves
3 allspice berries
2 tablespoons dried Mexican
  oregano
I sprig fresh thyme
I clove garlic, peeled
¼ cup chopped onion

2 tablespoons apple cider vinegar
6 to 8 ounces beef roast
Salt and pepper
2 dried avocado leaves
  (approximately 6 by 5 inches)
I flour tortilla
Beans, rice, or vegetables of your
  choice
Salsa, for serving

1. Put the guajillo pepper in a bowl and pour hot water over it to cover. Set aside for 20 minutes.

2. Grind the cumin seeds, cloves, and allspice in a spice grinder. Drain the guajillo pepper, remove the stem and any seeds, and transfer to a blender along with the ground spices. Add the oregano, thyme, garlic, onion, and vinegar with a little water and puree to a paste. Strain the mixture through a fine-mesh strainer.

3. Season the beef with salt and pepper. Rub all over with the spice paste and marinate for 4 hours, covered, in the refrigerator.

4. Preheat the oven to 325°F.

5. In a small roasting pan, place 1 of the avocado leaves on the bottom, put the meat on top of the leaf, and put the remaining leaf on top of the meat. Cover the pan tightly with foil and roast until the meat is fork tender, at least 1 hour, depending on the thickness. Discard the leaves. Shred the meat with a fork or pull apart with your hands.

6. Heat the flour tortilla and layer with the shredded meat and beans, rice, or vegetables of your choice. Roll up into a burrito and serve with salsa on the side.

Serves 1

AT-HOME COST: $10

Avocado leaves can be used fresh or dried, and if not readily available, they can be ordered online. Alternatively, you could use bay leaves layered with cracked anise seeds.

Guajillo peppers are brownish red in color with touches of gold-orange; this medium-hot pepper has a pleasantly tart, fruity taste. Ancho chiles can be substituted in this recipe.

CHIPOTLE MEXICAN GRILL

corn salsa

THIS ROASTED CORN AND CHILE SALSA IS GREAT AS A CONDIMENT FOR MEAT AND CHICKEN.

6 ears yellow corn (in husks)
2 poblano peppers
2 red jalapeño peppers
½ red onion

¼ cup chopped fresh cilantro
1 tablespoon lime juice
Salt and pepper

1. Grill the corn over a charcoal fire, turning often, until the first layer of husk is completely charred. Depending on your fire, this could take from 5 to 10 minutes. To remove the corn from its husk, cut the stem end up to the bottom of the ear and peel back the husks and silk. You may need to brush away burned silks.

2. Roast the poblanos on a grill over a charcoal fire, turning often, until the chiles are charred. Put the chiles in a bowl and cover with plastic wrap for about 15 minutes—the skin will blister in the steam. Remove the charred skins and seeds either under running water or in a bowl of water.

3. Cut the kernels of corn off the cobs. Cut the roasted poblanos, the jalapeños, and the red onion into small dice. Mix the corn, poblanos, jalapeños, onion, and cilantro together and season with the lime juice and salt and pepper to taste.

Makes about 5 cups

AT-HOME COST: $3

CLAIM JUMPER
pot roast and vegetables

TENDER BEEF AND ROASTED VEGETABLES IN AN HERB GRAVY, SERVED WITH MASHED POTATOES.

Vegetables
½ cup chopped carrots
½ cup chopped turnip
½ cup chopped sweet potato
1 medium onion, chopped
Assorted chopped fresh herbs
   (thyme, rosemary, oregano)
Olive oil
Salt and pepper

Herb Gravy
1 clove garlic, chopped
¼ cup chopped shallots

½ cup fresh herbs, chopped
2 tablespoons olive oil
1 cup beef broth or store-bought
   au jus mix (see Note)

Roast
12 ounces fully cooked chuck
   roast, cut into 1-inch cubes

Mashed potatoes, for serving

1. Do ahead: Preheat the oven to 375°F.

2. Roast the vegetables with the fresh herbs in a little olive oil until caramelized. Season with salt and pepper, then let cool and refrigerate in a covered container until ready to use.

3. Do ahead: To make the herb gravy, sauté the garlic, shallots, and fresh herbs in the olive oil. Add the beef broth and simmer for about 5 minutes; set aside.

4. Place the cubed meat in a skillet with the roasted vegetables and herb gravy and simmer just to heat through.

5. Serve with mashed potatoes.

Note: *Au jus* is a French term for meat served with its natural juices. French's makes a ready-mix variety.

AT-HOME COST: $7.50

The Claim Jumper chain of restaurants first opened in 1977, all with the theme of the California gold rush. Known for their large portions, this chain's menu has a wide variety of sandwiches, pizzas, and salads, with the main focus on steaks and ribs.

CLAIM JUMPER
roasted pork loin

ROASTED PORK SERVED WITH SEASONED POTATOES, SAUTÉED VEGETABLES, AND
A LIGHT GLAZE OF BARBECUE SAUCE, GARNISHED WITH TORTILLA STRIPS.

1 cup chopped mixed vegetables
1 tablespoon olive oil
¼ cup salsa
2 scoops mashed potatoes
¼ cup chopped roasted red
  peppers, homemade or
  store-bought
1 teaspoon chopped fresh cilantro

½ cup mixed grated Cheddar and
  Monterey Jack cheese
One 6- to 7-pound cooked pork
  loin
½ cup barbecue sauce
½ cup tortilla strips
2 biscuits

1. Steam the vegetables for 2 to 3 minutes, until crisp-tender. Set aside.

2. Heat the oil in a skillet and add the vegetables, sautéing for a few
   seconds. Add the salsa and heat through, then transfer to a bowl.

3. Combine the mashed potatoes, roasted peppers, cilantro, and mixed
   cheeses. Mix well with a wooden spoon or rubber spatula.

4. Top the vegetable mixture with the mashed potato mixture. Put a bowl
   of veggie-potato mix on each of 2 warmed plates. Place a serving of pork
   loin alongside the bowl, glaze with a little barbecue sauce, and top with
   the tortilla strips. Place a warm biscuit at the rim of the plate and serve
   immediately.

Serves 2

AT-HOME COST: $9.50

Make your own barbecue sauce, biscuits, and salsa from any of
the recipes in this book or save time by using store-bought items.

DAVE AND BUSTER'S
blackened chicken pasta

SAUTÉED CHICKEN SERVED IN A CAJUN ALFREDO SAUCE WITH TOMATOES AND MUSHROOMS ATOP LINGUINE.

Cajun Blackening Spice
¼ cup paprika
3 tablespoons garlic powder
2 tablespoons celery salt
1 tablespoon onion powder
1 tablespoon ground cumin
1 teaspoon cayenne pepper
1 teaspoon dried thyme
1 teaspoon chili powder

Chicken and Pasta Sauce
1 tablespoon olive oil
6 ounces boneless, skinless
  chicken breast, cut into
  bite-size pieces
1 cup sliced mushrooms
2 teaspoons Paul Prudhomme's
  Poultry Magic

1 teaspoon minced garlic
⅓ cup diced Roma tomatoes,
  plus extra for garnish
¼ cup Alfredo sauce, homemade
  or store-bought
1½ cups heavy cream
1½ tablespoons grated Asiago
  cheese

For Serving
8 ounces linguine, cooked
  according to the package
  directions
1 teaspoon chopped fresh
  parsley

1. Do ahead: Make the Cajun blackening spice by combining all the ingredients; store in a tightly covered container until ready to use. (This mix makes more than necessary for this recipe, so feel free to add some Louisiana heat to other dishes.)

2. Heat the oil in a skillet and sauté the chicken and mushrooms. Sprinkle with the Poultry Magic and cook the chicken all the way through. Add the garlic and diced tomatoes and sauté for another minute.

3. Lower the heat and add 2 teaspoons of the Cajun blackening spice, the Alfredo sauce, and the heavy cream. Stir well to combine the ingredients, then take the pan off the heat and add the Asiago cheese.

4. Portion the cooked linguine onto 2 warmed serving plates by using tongs and swirling and mounding the pasta onto each plate. Top with the chicken and sauce. Garnish with diced tomato and sprinkle with the chopped parsley.

Serves 2

AT-HOME COST: $7.50

Make substitutions for the pasta based on what you have on hand—bow-tie and penne work just as well as the linguine.

A visit to Dave and Buster's is unique. The concept, which came to fruition in Dallas in 1982, is a mixture of food and fun—enjoy playing arcade games, pinball, pool, and other games before or after enjoying their fabulous menu of burgers, steaks, finger foods, and salads.

DAVE AND BUSTER'S
cheddar mashed potatoes

JUST THE RIGHT MIX OF CREAMY POTATOES, A HINT OF GARLIC, AND TASTY
CHEDDAR CHEESE.

Garlic Butter
1 teaspoon minced garlic
1 tablespoon olive oil
8 tablespoons (1 stick) butter,
  softened
1 teaspoon chopped fresh
  parsley

Potatoes
2 pounds red potatoes, scrubbed
  and cut into 1-inch chunks
1/3 cup heavy cream
4 ounces white Cheddar or
  Monterey Jack cheese, shredded
Salt and pepper

1. Do ahead: Make the garlic butter by lightly sautéing the garlic in the olive oil—it should get soft but not brown. Add the softened butter and parsley, then gently whisk everything together, pour into a covered container, and refrigerate until ready to use.

2. Cook the potatoes in salted boiling water until they are soft, 5 to 10 minutes, then drain well. Place them in a warmed serving bowl and add the cream, cheese, and 1/4 cup of the garlic butter. Mash with a fork or beat very lightly with a hand mixer, then season with salt and pepper to taste.

Serves 4

AT-HOME COST: $3

Double or triple the recipe for garlic butter, refrigerate, and use it to flavor grilled meat and fish.

DAVE AND BUSTER'S
steak fajita salad

FAJITA-FLAVORED GRILLED STEAK TOPS A SALAD OF HEARTS OF ROMAINE, CHEESE, ONION, AND TORTILLA STRIPS TOSSED WITH A BUTTERMILK-CILANTRO DRESSING.

Buttermilk-Cilantro Dressing
One 1-ounce package buttermilk
 ranch salad dressing mix
½ cup mayonnaise
½ cup sour cream
¼ cup buttermilk
1 cup chopped fresh cilantro
2 cloves garlic, minced
¼ teaspoon cayenne pepper, or to
 taste

Salad
8 ounces steak
One 1.12-ounce package fajita
 seasoning mix

6 ounces romaine hearts,
 chopped
½ cup grated Cheddar cheese
¼ cup diced onion
1 cup plain tortilla strips
1 large flour tortilla bowl
 (see page 64)

Garnish
Sour cream
Multicolored tortilla strips
2 tablespoons chopped fresh
 cilantro

1. Do ahead: Combine all the ingredients for the buttermilk-cilantro dressing in a blender and process until smooth. Refrigerate in a covered container until ready to use.

2. Follow the package directions to marinate the steak in the fajita seasoning mix.

3. Light a charcoal grill or preheat the broiler.

4. Drain the steak from the marinade and grill or broil to the desired doneness. Slice it against the grain into even strips. Discard the marinade.

5. Toss the romaine with the cheese, onion, and the plain tortilla strips. Combine with 6 tablespoons of the salad dressing and fill the tortilla

bowl. Top with the strips of steak. Garnish with sour cream, multicolored tortilla strips, and the cilantro.

Serves 2

AT-HOME COST: $6.50

Substitute fat-free mayonnaise and sour cream, and low-fat buttermilk.

Substitute chicken or turkey for the beef.

DON PABLO'S
chicken nachos

A PLATTER OF CHICKEN AND REFRIED BEANS OVER TORTILLA CHIPS, TOPPED WITH CHEESE AND SERVED WITH SOUR CREAM AND HOT JALAPEÑO.

10 large flat tortilla chips	Shredded lettuce
¾ cup shredded Cheddar cheese	1 tablespoon sliced jalapeño pepper
½ cup refried beans	¼ cup sour cream
½ cup chopped cooked chicken	3 tablespoons diced tomatoes

1. Layer the chips on a warmed large serving platter and sprinkle with half the Cheddar cheese. Spoon the warmed beans over the cheese, then top with the cooked chicken and finish with the remaining cheese.

2. Place the lettuce on one side of the platter and layer the jalapeño slices on top. Garnish the nachos with dollops of sour cream and finish with the diced tomatoes.

Serves 2

AT-HOME COST: $5.50

Substitute cooked steak or beef in place of the chicken.

Omit the chips and serve on a bed of chopped lettuce, adding additional tomatoes or salsa; use a low-fat or fat-free sour cream.

Since 1986, Don Pablo's restaurants have been serving customers their made-from-scratch salsa, tortillas, fajitas, enchiladas, burritos, combination platters, special recipe sauces, and a wide range of Tex-Mex specialty items.

DON PABLO'S
queso dip

A WARM BLEND OF MELTED CHEESE, CHILE PEPPERS, ONION, AND TOMATOES SERVED WITH TORTILLA CHIPS.

3 tablespoons butter
1 cup chopped onion
One 20-ounce can Ro*Tel diced tomatoes with green chiles, with juice
One 14.5-ounce can stewed tomatoes, chopped, with juice

2 pounds processed cheese such as Velveeta, cubed
1 pound sharp Cheddar cheese, cubed
Tortilla chips, for serving

1. Heat the butter in a large saucepan and lightly sauté the onion until soft. Add both cans of tomatoes and simmer until thickened.

2. Add the cheeses to the tomato mixture and stir, over medium heat, until the cheese is melted and smooth. Let cool, then refrigerate overnight in a covered container. Gently reheat before serving with tortilla chips.

Serves 6 to 8

AT-HOME COST: $9

Ro*Tel is a nationally recognized brand of canned goods. You may use another brand of diced tomatoes with green chiles if Ro*Tel is not available in your market.

EMERIL'S NEW ORLEANS RESTAURANT
barbecued shrimp

SHRIMP SEASONED AS ONLY EMERIL CAN DO IT! SERVED IN A CREAMY BARBECUE SAUCE.

Emeril's Original Essence
2½ tablespoons paprika
2 tablespoons salt
2 tablespoons garlic powder
1 tablespoon black pepper
2 tablespoons onion powder
1 tablespoon cayenne pepper
1 tablespoon dried oregano
1 tablespoon dried thyme

Barbecue Sauce Base
1 tablespoon vegetable oil
½ cup chopped onion
1 teaspoon salt
1 teaspoon coarsely ground black pepper
3 bay leaves

1 tablespoon minced garlic
3 lemons, peeled and quartered, white pith removed
½ cup dry white wine
2 cups shrimp broth (see Note)
1 cup Worcestershire sauce

Shrimp
2 pounds medium shrimp, peeled and deveined, with tails left intact
½ teaspoon black pepper
1 tablespoon vegetable oil
1 cup heavy cream
2 tablespoons unsalted butter, cut into pieces

1. Do ahead: Make Emeril's Original Essence by combining all the spices. Whisk together well and store in a covered container until ready to use. This mix makes more than is necessary for this recipe, so feel free to add a little "Bam!" to other dishes.

2. Do ahead: For the barbecue sauce base, heat the oil and sauté the onion, salt, black pepper, and bay leaves over high heat. Stir constantly so that the ingredients don't burn—the onion should be soft. Add the garlic, lemons, and wine, and simmer for about 2 minutes. Add the shrimp

broth (or substitute) and the Worcestershire sauce, then bring the mixture to a boil. Reduce the heat and simmer until the mixture is reduced to ½ cup, about 1 hour. Stir occasionally so the sauce doesn't burn. When thickened, pass the sauce through a fine-mesh strainer, pushing on the solids with a spoon to release as much liquid as possible. Let the mixture cool, then refrigerate in a covered container until ready to use.

3. Do ahead: Season the shrimp with 1 tablespoon of Emeril's Original Essence and the ½ teaspoon black pepper. Refrigerate until ready to cook.

4. To cook the shrimp, heat the vegetable oil in a large skillet. Add the shrimp and cook, stirring, until they begin to turn pink, about 2 minutes. Add the heavy cream and ¼ cup of the barbecue sauce base, and simmer over medium heat until the sauce is reduced by half, about 3 minutes. Do not let the shrimp overcook, or they will be tough. Once they are cooked, transfer them with tongs or a slotted spoon to a warmed platter.

5. Remove the pan from the heat and whisk in the pieces of butter, one by one, until they are all incorporated and the sauce has a smooth consistency. Pour the sauce over the cooked shrimp and serve.

Note: Substitute bottled clam juice for the shrimp broth, or use half clam juice and half water or vegetable broth.

Serves 4 to 6

AT-HOME COST: $9

Emeril's New Orleans Restaurant features fine Cajun/Creole/Louisiana cuisine from celebrity chef Emeril Lagasse. The restaurant's innovative design has a Food Bar framed by a tapestry of glass-encased spices showcasing the bold and creative flavors that Chef Emeril features, and a state-of-the-art kitchen that is visible from the main dining room.

EMERIL'S NEW ORLEANS RESTAURANT

rosemary biscuits

WHIP UP A BATCH OF THESE WONDERFUL BISCUITS TO SERVE WITH EMERIL'S NEW ORLEANS RESTAURANT BARBECUED SHRIMP (PAGE 88).

1 cup all-purpose flour, plus extra for dusting
1 teaspoon baking powder
½ teaspoon salt
⅛ teaspoon baking soda
3 tablespoons cold unsalted butter, cut into small pieces
1 tablespoon minced fresh rosemary, or 1 teaspoon dried
½ to ¾ cup buttermilk

1. Preheat the oven to 450°F.

2. In a large bowl, mix together the dry ingredients, whisking to blend thoroughly. Cut in the butter, using a pastry cutter or 2 dinner knives, until the mixture resembles coarse crumbs. Add the minced rosemary. Pour in ½ cup buttermilk and gently stir with a wooden spoon until the dough is just mixed—do not overmix, as this will make the biscuits tough. If the dough seems too dry, add a little more buttermilk. Gently form into a dough ball.

3. Flour a work surface such as a cutting board, and pat the dough ball out to a circle about 7 inches in diameter and ½ inch thick. Using a 1-inch round cookie cutter, cut the biscuits and place on a baking sheet. Make sure to leave plenty of room in between the biscuits.

4. Bake for 10 to 12 minutes, until the biscuits are lightly golden brown on the top and the bottom. Serve warm.

Makes 12 mini biscuits

AT-HOME COST: $2.50

FAMOUS DAVE'S
firecracker chicken wings

FAMOUS DAVE'S AWARD-WINNING WINGS, UNIQUELY SEASONED AND TOSSED IN THEIR DEVIL'S SPIT HOT SAUCE.

Famous Dave's Dragon Wing Dust

2 tablespoons anise seeds

2 tablespoons salt

2 tablespoons Chinese five-spice powder

3 tablespoons superfine sugar

I tablespoon paprika

I tablespoon garlic seasoning

2 teaspoons cayenne pepper

2 teaspoons black pepper

I teaspoon garlic powder

Wings

24 chicken wings

2 cups chicken marinade, homemade or store-bought

Peanut oil, for frying

All-purpose flour, for coating the wings

8 tablespoons (I stick) butter, melted

Famous Dave's Devil's Spit hot sauce

Sweet-and-sour sauce, for serving

1. Do ahead: Make Famous Dave's Dragon Wing Dust. In a spice grinder, grind the anise seeds to a fine powder. Combine with the remaining dust ingredients and grind. Store in a covered container.

2. Marinate the wings in the marinade of your choice for 4 hours in the refrigerator. Drain the wings and discard the marinade. Heat ¾ inch of peanut oil to 375°F. Toss the wings in flour; shake off the excess. Working in batches, fry the wings until they are golden brown and cooked through. Transfer to a baking sheet.

3. Mix the melted butter and hot sauce. With a pastry brush, coat each of the wings, then sprinkle generously with the Dragon Wing Dust. Serve with sweet-and-sour sauce.

Serves 4 as an appetizer

AT-HOME COST: $6.50

Devil's Spit is available online at Famous Dave's website, famousbbqstore.com. You can also substitute Tabasco sauce.

You can use chicken legs, thighs, or breast tenders in this recipe.

Dave Anderson's lifelong passion for perfecting his barbecue ribs and recipes has garnered him many national awards for the best ribs and the best sauces in America. He opened his first Famous Dave's in Chicago, in 1996.

FAMOUS DAVE'S
crossroads delta black beans

BLACK BEANS WITH HAM, LOADED WITH A ZESTY FLAVOR AS ONLY FAMOUS DAVE'S CAN.

Beans
2 pounds dried black beans
3 quarts chicken broth
2 medium green bell peppers, cut into quarters
4 bay leaves
2 pounds smoked ham hocks
¼ teaspoon cayenne pepper
½ bunch fresh cilantro, coarsely chopped

Vegetables
½ cup bacon drippings
2 medium onions, chopped
1 medium green bell pepper, chopped

1 medium red bell pepper, chopped
2 large jalapeño peppers, finely minced
2 tablespoons chopped fresh basil
1 tablespoon ground cumin
¼ cup minced garlic

2 tablespoons Famous Dave's Barbecue Sauce (page 95; see Note)
2 tablespoons Kahlúa
2 teaspoons lime juice
1 teaspoon kosher salt

For serving
8 cups cooked rice

1. Do ahead: Pick through the beans, discarding any that are broken and checking for small stones. Put the beans in a large stockpot with the chicken broth, bell peppers, bay leaves, ham hocks, and cayenne. Bring to a simmer and skim off the foam that comes from the ham hocks. Stir in the cilantro and simmer, covered, for 1½ to 2 hours, until the beans are tender. Check often for liquid, making sure it doesn't cook away. When the beans are tender, remove and discard the bay leaves and peppers. Remove the meat from the ham hocks and discard the bones. Dice the meat, then return it to the pot.

2. Heat ¼ cup of the bacon drippings and sauté the onions, bell peppers, and jalapeños—the vegetables should be soft, not browned. Add the basil and cumin, then remove from the heat and set aside.

3. In a separate skillet, heat the remaining ¼ cup bacon drippings and sauté the garlic, stirring frequently, until it is golden brown.

4. Drain the beans and reserve the cooking liquid; set the beans aside in the stockpot. Add the sautéed vegetable mixture and the sautéed garlic to the bean cooking liquid. Add the barbecue sauce, Kahlúa, lime juice, and salt. Transfer the mixture to a blender and puree. Return the puree to the stockpot with the beans and ham hock meat. Simmer for about 5 minutes, stirring occasionally, then remove from the heat. Refrigerate in a covered container overnight. Gently reheat before serving over the rice.

Note: Make Famous Dave's Barbecue Sauce from the recipe provided in this book, or use a brand you are familiar with. You can buy Famous Dave's Sweet & Zesty BBQ Sauce at famousbbqstore.com

Serves 8

AT-HOME COST: $8.50

You can substitute solid shortening or lard for the bacon drippings.

FAMOUS DAVE'S
barbecue sauce

THE SAUCE THAT MADE DAVE FAMOUS: SWEET AND TANGY, WITH PLENTY OF SURPRISE INGREDIENTS.

2 slices thick-cut hickory-smoked bacon, chopped
¼ cup chopped onion
¾ cup peach schnapps
½ cup raisins
1 large jalapeño pepper, finely diced
2 cloves garlic, minced
⅓ cup Alessi balsamic vinegar
¼ cup chopped apple
¼ cup frozen tangerine juice concentrate or orange juice concentrate
¼ cup frozen pineapple juice concentrate
3 tablespoons dark molasses
2 tablespoons apple cider vinegar

2 tablespoons lemon juice
2 tablespoons lime juice
2¼ cups dark corn syrup
One 12-ounce can tomato paste
½ cup packed light brown sugar
½ cup Worcestershire sauce
2 tablespoons yellow mustard
2 teaspoons chili powder
1 teaspoon Maggi seasoning
1 teaspoon salt
½ teaspoon red pepper flakes
¼ teaspoon coarsely ground black pepper
1 teaspoon cayenne pepper
¼ cup Kahlúa
1 teaspoon liquid smoke

1. Do ahead: In a large saucepan over medium heat, sauté the bacon to render the fat (save the bacon bits for another use). You should have 1 tablespoon of bacon drippings. Sauté the onion in the bacon fat until it is caramelized to a dark golden brown. Reduce the heat to low and deglaze the saucepan with ¼ cup of water. Stir in the peach schnapps, then add the raisins, jalapeño, and garlic. Simmer, stirring occasionally, for about 20 minutes, or until the mixture is the consistency of syrup. Remove from the heat and set aside, or let cool and refrigerate in a covered container until ready to use.

2. Transfer the onion mixture to a blender and add the balsamic vinegar, chopped apple, tangerine and pineapple juice concentrates, molasses,

apple cider vinegar, and lemon and lime juices. Process until pureed, and return to the saucepan. Add the corn syrup, tomato paste, light brown sugar, Worcestershire sauce, mustard, chili powder, Maggi seasoning, salt, red pepper flakes, black pepper, and cayenne pepper. Simmer over low heat for about 20 minutes, stirring occasionally. Remove from the heat and stir in the Kahlúa and liquid smoke. Let cool, then refrigerate in a covered container until ready to use.

Makes about 10 cups

AT-HOME COST: $5.50

Substitute another brand for the Alessi balsamic vinegar if Alessi brand is not available. Substitute peach nectar in place of the peach schnapps if you would prefer not to use alcohol.

Maggi seasoning is a vegetable protein extract that is added to soups, stews, casseroles, dips, etc., as a flavor booster and can be found in the spice aisle.

FAMOUS DAVE'S
shakin' the shack potato salad

MADE WITH RED ONION, CELERY, HARD-COOKED EGGS, MAYONNAISE, AND A HINT OF MUSTARD.

3 pounds russet potatoes, scrubbed
1¼ cups mayonnaise
½ cup sour cream
1 tablespoon yellow mustard
1 tablespoon white vinegar
1 teaspoon salt
1 teaspoon sugar
½ teaspoon pepper

½ cup minced celery
½ cup minced red onion
½ cup minced green bell pepper
2 tablespoons minced pimiento
1 tablespoon minced jalapeño pepper
5 hard-cooked eggs, minced
¼ cup pickle relish
Paprika, for garnish

1. Do ahead: Put the potatoes in a pot and cover with water. Boil until they are tender and cooked through but not mushy. Drain and refrigerate until cold.

2. In a large bowl, combine the mayonnaise, sour cream, mustard, vinegar, salt, sugar, and pepper and refrigerate until ready to use.

3. Peel the skins from the cold potatoes and coarsely chop them.

4. Combine the celery, red onion, bell pepper, pimiento, and jalapeño. Add to the mayonnaise mixture, then fold in the potatoes, eggs, and relish. Garnish with paprika.

Serves 6 to 8

AT-HOME COST: $5.50

FAMOUS DAVE'S
route 66 truck stop chili

CHILI WITH FAMOUS DAVE'S FLAIR AND A BIT OF A ZING!

1 1/2 pounds coarsely ground beef
1 teaspoon Famous Dave's Steak
  and Burger Seasoning (see Note)
3 1/2 tablespoons chili powder
1/2 teaspoon coarsely ground
  pepper
2 teaspoons ground cumin
1 1/2 teaspoons dried basil
1/2 teaspoon garlic powder
1 teaspoon Maggi seasoning
1/2 cup chopped celery
1/2 cup chopped onion, plus extra
  for garnish
1/2 cup chopped green bell pepper
1/2 jalapeño pepper, minced

One 16-ounce can hot chili beans,
  with sauce
1/2 (22-ounce) can tomato juice
1/2 (15-ounce) can diced tomatoes,
  with juice
1/2 (15-ounce) can tomato puree
1/2 (10-ounce) can beef broth
1 1/2 tablespoons Famous Dave's
  Barbecue Sauce (page 95)
1 tablespoon Kahlúa
1 tablespoon Worcestershire sauce

Shredded Cheddar cheese, for
  garnish
Crackers, for serving

1. Sauté the ground beef with the steak and burger seasoning, chili powder, pepper, cumin, basil, garlic powder, and Maggi seasoning in a large pot, such as a Dutch oven, over medium heat until the beef is well browned, stirring frequently. Add the celery, onion, bell pepper, and jalapeño, and sauté until the vegetables are soft. Then add the remaining chili ingredients and simmer until the liquid thickens.

2. Let cool, then refrigerate overnight in a covered container to allow the flavors to blend. Reheat gently before serving.

3. Garnish with shredded Cheddar and chopped onion; serve with crackers.

Note: Famous Dave's Steak and Burger Seasoning is available online at the Famous Dave's website, famousbbqstore.com.

AT-HOME COST: $9.85

Substitute ground turkey or chicken for the beef in this recipe.

Maggi seasoning is a vegetable protein extract that is added to soups, stews, casseroles, dips, etc., as a flavor booster and can be found in the spice aisle.

FAMOUS DAVE'S
'que sandwiches

FAMOUS DAVE'S 'QUE SANDWICHES COVER THE FOUR BARBECUE FOOD GROUPS:
SMOKED MEAT, SEASONED MEAT, SLICED MEAT, AND LOTS OF MEAT. EAT UP!

1 pound ground beef	¼ teaspoon cayenne pepper
½ cup minced onion	1½ cups Famous Dave's Barbecue
¼ cup minced green bell pepper	Sauce (page 95)
1 jalapeño pepper, minced	1 teaspoon yellow mustard
1 teaspoon Famous Dave's Steak	4 hamburger buns, split in half,
and Burger Seasoning (see Note)	toasted, and buttered
1 tablespoon chili powder	

1. Crumble the ground beef and sauté over high heat until brown. Drain the fat and add the onion, bell pepper, jalapeño, steak and burger seasoning, and chili powder, stirring frequently.

2. When the beef is thoroughly cooked, add the cayenne, barbecue sauce, and mustard. Simmer for about 5 minutes, or until all the flavors have blended.

3. Spoon a portion of the barbecue beef onto the bottom half of each of the buns and cover with the top half. Enjoy with lots of napkins!

Serves 4

AT-HOME COST: $7

Note: Famous Dave's Steak and Burger Seasoning is available online at the Famous Dave's website, famousbbqstore.com.

FAMOUS DAVE'S
voodoo chicken

MARINATED CHICKEN BREASTS COATED IN FAMOUS DAVE'S CAJUN DYNAMITE DUST, SERVED WITH THEIR BLACK BEANS AND THEIR MOJO SALSA.

4 boneless, skinless chicken breasts
1 cup Italian dressing, homemade or store-bought
¼ cup Famous Dave's Cajun Dynamite Dust (page 102)
1 tablespoon butter

¼ cup Whoop That Sweet Thang sweet-and-sour sauce, or another brand of your choice
4 cups cooked rice
4 cups Famous Dave's Crossroads Delta Black Beans (page 93)
Famous Dave's Mojo Salsa, for serving (page 103)

1. Do ahead: Marinate the chicken breasts in the Italian dressing in the refrigerator for at least 2 hours. Use a resealable plastic bag, and give the chicken an occasional light massage.

2. Remove the chicken from the marinade and shake off the excess. Put the Cajun Dynamite Dust on a plate and coat both sides of each breast with the dust.

3. Use a cast-iron skillet to cook the chicken, if you have one. Heat the skillet over high heat and add the butter—it will melt quickly. Add the chicken breasts and sauté until they are blackened and cooked through (no longer pink in the middle), turning once. Brush both sides with the sweet-and-sour sauce and transfer the chicken to a warmed platter.

4. Place 1 cup of hot rice on each plate, top with 1 cup of the black beans, and put 1 chicken breast on top of the beans. Serve with Famous Dave's Mojo Salsa.

Serves 4

AT-HOME COST: $9.75

FAMOUS DAVE'S

cajun dynamite dust

THIS SEASONING IS USED AS A RUB FOR BLACKENED BEEF, CHICKEN, AND
SHRIMP.

½ cup paprika

¼ cup plus 2 tablespoons kosher
  salt

¼ cup coarsely ground black
  pepper

3 tablespoons dried basil

3 tablespoons filé powder

3 tablespoons garlic powder

2 tablespoons onion powder

2 tablespoons dried oregano

2 tablespoons cayenne pepper

2 tablespoons white pepper

2 tablespoons dried thyme

Whisk all the ingredients together and store in a covered container.

Makes 2 cups

AT-HOME COST: $4.25

Filé (pronounced FEE-lay) powder is made from ground sassafras
leaves. It is used in gumbo as a thickener, but it is also used for its
flavor. It might not be available in local markets, but there are several
online sources.

FAMOUS DAVE'S
mojo salsa

A CAJUN-STYLE SALSA TO COMPLEMENT JUST ABOUT ANY DISH.

2 tablespoons butter
⅓ cup minced green, red, and
   yellow bell peppers
⅓ cup chopped red onion
1 cup canned black beans, drained
1 cup frozen corn kernels
¼ cup frozen tangerine juice
   concentrate or orange juice
   concentrate
1 large jalapeño pepper, minced

2 tablespoons lime juice
1 tablespoon chopped fresh
   cilantro
1 teaspoon red pepper flakes
¼ teaspoon salt
¼ teaspoon coarsely ground black
   pepper
2 medium bananas, chopped
One 8-ounce can pineapple chunks,
   drained

Heat the butter in a large skillet and sauté the bell peppers and onion until the onion is soft. Add the beans, corn, tangerine juice concentrate, jalapeño, lime juice, cilantro, red pepper flakes, salt, and black pepper. Simmer for a few minutes, then stir in the bananas and pineapple. Let cool, then store in a covered container.

Makes 4 cups

AT-HOME COST: $5.50

GARIBALDI CAFE

chicken rigatoni

RIGATONI PASTA, CHICKEN, AND MUSHROOMS IN A CREAM SAUCE.

½ cup diced onion
1 tablespoon clarified butter (see page 42)
¼ cup sliced shiitake mushrooms
¼ cup Marsala wine
¼ cup chicken broth
¼ cup plus 2 tablespoons heavy cream

3 ounces Parmesan cheese, grated, plus extra for garnish
6 ounces chicken breast, cooked and shredded
4 ounces rigatoni pasta, cooked according to the package directions

1. Sauté the onion in the clarified butter and cook for 2 minutes, then add the mushrooms and cook for another minute.

2. Deglaze the pan with the Marsala and reduce the liquid by half. Add the broth, cream, and Parmesan cheese. Bring to a simmer and stir frequently to keep the cheese from sticking to the bottom of the pan. Add the shredded chicken and warm through.

3. Toss the warm pasta with the chicken and sauce; garnish with extra Parmesan cheese.

Serves 1

AT-HOME COST: $4

If Marsala isn't available, use dry sherry instead.

Since 1978, Garibaldi Cafe in Charleston, South Carolina, has been known for Italian-style pasta, veal, chicken, seafood, and steak.

GARIBALDI CAFE
clam linguine

LINGUINE IN A BUTTER-CREAM SAUCE WITH FRESH LITTLENECK CLAMS.

2 tablespoons butter
½ clove garlic, minced
½ shallot, diced
3 littleneck clams, scrubbed under running water (see Note)
¼ cup white wine
2 tablespoons lemon juice
¼ cup chicken broth or fish broth
¼ cup heavy cream
½ teaspoon chopped fresh thyme
2 dashes of Tabasco sauce
4 ounces linguine pasta, cooked according to the package directions
1 tablespoon grated Parmesan cheese, for garnish
Pinch of chopped fresh parsley, for garnish

1. Heat the butter in a skillet and sauté the garlic and shallot until soft—do not let the butter get brown. When the butter begins to bubble, add the clams and cook, covered, over medium-low heat for 3 to 5 minutes. Shake the pan frequently so the clams move around. Add the wine, lemon juice, and broth; cover and simmer for 2 to 3 minutes more, until the clams open up.

2. Add the cream, thyme, and Tabasco sauce and cook until the liquid is reduced by half, 3 to 5 minutes.

3. Add the linguine to the pan and toss with the clams and sauce. Using tongs, mound the pasta on a warmed plate and put the clams around the plate.

4. Garnish with the Parmesan cheese and parsley.

Note: If the clams are small, add 3 more to the recipe.

Serves 1

AT-HOME COST: $3.50

GOLDEN CORRAL
bourbon street chicken

MARINATED CHICKEN IN A BOURBON-GINGER SAUCE.

½ cup soy sauce
½ cup packed dark brown sugar
½ teaspoon garlic powder
1 teaspoon ground ginger
2 tablespoons onion flakes

½ cup Jim Beam bourbon, or
  another brand of your choice
1 pound chicken leg or thigh meat,
  cut into bite-size pieces
2 tablespoons white wine

1. Do ahead: Whisk together the soy sauce, brown sugar, garlic powder, ginger, onion flakes, and bourbon. Pour over the chicken pieces in a bowl and marinate in the refrigerator for 4 hours, stirring occasionally.

2. Preheat the oven to 350°F.

3. Transfer the chicken to a baking pan and arrange in a single layer. Pour any marinade left in the bowl over the chicken pieces and bake for 1 hour, stirring and basting with the marinade about every 10 minutes.

4. When the chicken is cooked through, transfer it to a plate and keep warm. If you used a metal baking pan, place it over a stovetop burner and deglaze the pan with the white wine, scraping up all the browned bits and the pan juices over medium-low heat. If you used a glass or ceramic dish, transfer the contents of the dish to a skillet and add the white wine.

5. Add the chicken to the baking pan or skillet and simmer for 5 minutes; serve warm.

Serves 4

AT-HOME COST: $5

The Golden Corral chain of family-style restaurants had its beginning in Fayetteville, North Carolina, in 1973. It still features large buffets and grilled items as well as a fabulous selection of desserts from its Brass Bell Bakery.

GOLDEN CORRAL
rolls

THESE DELICIOUS, FEATHER-LIGHT ROLLS GO WELL WITH JUST ABOUT ANY
MEAL.

1 envelope (2¼ teaspoons) active
  dry yeast
¼ cup warm water (105° to 115°F)
⅓ cup sugar
6 tablespoons (¾ stick) unsalted
  butter, plus extra for the pan

1 teaspoon salt
1 cup hot milk
1 egg, beaten
4½ cups all-purpose flour, sifted

1. In a large bowl, sprinkle the yeast over the warm water and let it proof, about 5 minutes.

2. In another bowl, combine the sugar, 4 tablespoons of the butter, the salt, and hot milk. Stir with a wooden spoon until the butter is melted and the sugar is dissolved. Let the mixture cool to 105° to 115°F, then add it to the proofed yeast mixture along with the beaten egg.

3. Add the flour 1 cup at a time, mixing well after each addition. After the fourth cup, form the dough into a soft ball. Sprinkle some of the remaining ½ cup flour onto a work surface and knead the dough for about 5 minutes, gradually working in all the remaining flour. Lightly grease the inside of a bowl and put the dough in it, turning it over once to grease all sides. Cover it with a damp towel and set the bowl in a warm area free from drafts.

4. When the dough has doubled in size, 1 to 1½ hours, punch it down and turn it out onto a lightly floured work surface and knead for 4 to 5 minutes. Butter an 18 by 13-inch baking pan and set aside.

5. Pinch off small chunks of dough and shape them into balls 1½ to 1¾ inches across until you have 24 rolls. Place the rolls in the prepared baking pan so that they do not touch each other. Cover with a damp towel and let rise in a warm, draft-free place until doubled in bulk, 30 to 40 minutes.

6. Preheat the oven to 375°F.

7. Melt the remaining 2 tablespoons butter. Using a pastry brush, brush the tops of the risen rolls with the melted butter and bake for 18 to 20 minutes, until they are browned on top.

Makes 24 rolls

AT-HOME COST: $2.50

GOLDEN CORRAL
seafood salad

THIS DELICIOUS CRAB-AND-SHRIMP SALAD CAN BE SERVED AS AN ENTRÉE ON A BED OF LETTUCE OR STUFFED IN SPLIT CROISSANTS.

8 ounces imitation crabmeat, shredded

I cup small shrimp, peeled, deveined, and cooked

I large green bell pepper, minced

I medium onion, minced

½ cup ranch salad dressing (Hidden Valley or another brand of your choice)

¼ cup mayonnaise

Lettuce leaves, for plate liners

Gently combine all the salad ingredients and refrigerate for about 1 hour. Mound on lettuce-lined salad plates for serving.

Serves 4 to 8

AT-HOME COST: $8.50

Substitute lobster meat for the imitation crab. For a nice variation, add a chopped hard-cooked egg and some Old Bay Seasoning for additional texture and flavor.

This recipe would also make an appetizing seafood cocktail mounded into martini glasses. Substituting some red bell pepper for part of the green bell pepper gives additional color for a nice presentation.

HARD ROCK CAFE
alfredo sauce

THE PERFECT CREAMY CHEESE SAUCE TO TOSS WITH YOUR FAVORITE PASTA.

4 tablespoons (½ stick) butter, melted
¼ cup all-purpose flour
4 cups heavy cream
1½ teaspoons dried basil
1½ teaspoons dried oregano
¼ teaspoon white pepper
¾ teaspoon salt
½ teaspoon ground nutmeg
1½ teaspoons chicken bouillon powder
½ cup grated Parmesan cheese

1. Do ahead: Make a roux in a small saucepan by combining the melted butter and the flour. Stir together over low heat until the mixture begins to color just a bit. Set aside.

2. Heat the cream with the basil, oregano, white pepper, salt, nutmeg, and bouillon powder and let it come to a quick boil. Whisk in the roux until it is completely incorporated, lower the heat, and let the mixture thicken, whisking frequently.

3. Add the Parmesan cheese, stirring until it is melted. Make sure it does not stick to the bottom of the pan. You can save this sauce for a later time. Let it cool, then refrigerate it in a covered container. Reheat very gently over low heat while stirring, and let it simmer for a few minutes before tossing with your favorite pasta.

Serves 4 to 6

AT-HOME COST: $4.85

If you want to avoid using flour, make a paste from 2 tablespoons of cornstarch and 5 tablespoons of water. Whisk them together and add as much as you need to the melted butter to achieve your desired thickness. You can make more roux than you need for this recipe.

Any extra can be covered with plastic wrap and refrigerated. Bring it to room temperature before using.

Hard Rock Cafe was started in 1971 in London as a "specialty theme" restaurant catering to rock 'n' roll lovers worldwide. The chain has become the world's leading collector and exhibitor of rock 'n' roll memorabilia, which can be seen on display in its restaurants. All this and great food as well.

HARD ROCK CAFE
baby back watermelon ribs

HARD ROCK'S FAMOUS SMOKEHOUSE RIBS, CHARRED JUST RIGHT AND SMOTHERED IN THEIR AUTHENTIC WATERMELON BARBECUE SAUCE.

Watermelon Barbecue Sauce
½ small seedless watermelon
1 cup dark corn syrup
¼ cup ketchup
¼ cup white vinegar

¾ teaspoon red pepper flakes
½ teaspoon liquid smoke
¼ teaspoon black pepper

4 racks baby back ribs (about 6 to 8 pounds)

1. Do ahead: Make the watermelon barbecue sauce. Remove the skin and about ½ inch of the white rind from the watermelon. You should be left with the tender part of the rind that is closest to the actual pulp. Cut the melon into chunks and puree in a blender for about 10 seconds. Drain the liquid out and measure the pulp—you should have about 1 cup of drained pulp.

2. Combine the pulp and the remaining ingredients in a saucepan and bring to a boil; then reduce the heat and simmer, covered, for about 1 hour, or until the mixture is a sauce consistency. Let the sauce cool, and refrigerate in a covered container until ready to use.

3. To make the ribs: Marinate the 4 racks of baby back ribs in the watermelon barbecue sauce (reserve some for basting and serving) for at least 2 hours, but preferably overnight, in the refrigerator.

4. Preheat the oven to 300°F.

5. Wrap the marinated ribs in foil and bake for 2 to 2½ hours, until the meat is falling off the bones. Just before serving, light a charcoal grill and char the ribs, basting often with the barbecue sauce. Serve the reserved sauce on the side.

Serves 4

AT-HOME COST: $9

Start marinating the ribs a day before you need them—the ribs will absorb more of the barbecue flavors.

HARD ROCK CAFE
blackened chicken penne pasta

CAJUN-SEASONED GRILLED CHICKEN BREAST SERVED OVER PENNE PASTA IN ALFREDO SAUCE.

Marinade

2 tablespoons lemon juice

2 tablespoons soy sauce

1 tablespoon lime juice

1 tablespoon Worcestershire sauce

8 ounces boneless, skinless chicken breast

Cajun Chicken Seasoning Mix

½ cup kosher salt

½ cup garlic pepper

½ cup white pepper

2 teaspoons cayenne pepper

1 teaspoon onion powder

8 ounces penne pasta, cooked according to the package directions

¾ cup Hard Rock Cafe Alfredo Sauce (page 112)

¾ cup baby spinach leaves

¼ cup tomatoes, diced

1 tablespoon grated Parmesan cheese

1 tablespoon chopped fresh parsley, for garnish

1 or 2 slices garlic toast, cut into 4 or 6 pieces, for serving

1   To make the marinade, combine all the ingredients with 2 cups water.

2.   Do ahead: Marinate the chicken breast, in the refrigerator, for at least 4 hours, or overnight.

3.   Do ahead: Make the Cajun seasoning mix by whisking all the ingredients together. Store in a covered container until ready to use.

4.   Light a charcoal grill or preheat the broiler. Remove the chicken from the marinade and season both sides with the Cajun seasoning. Discard the marinade. Grill until cooked through and no longer pink in the middle, turning once. When cool enough to handle, cut into 5 or 6 slices.

5.   Toss the penne with the Alfredo sauce and add the spinach and tomatoes and heat through. Transfer to a warmed serving bowl and add the sliced

chicken. Sprinkle with the Parmesan cheese and garnish with the chopped parsley.

6. Position the garlic toast around the inside rim of the bowl and serve warm.

Serves 2

AT-HOME COST: $6.00

Search the spice aisle of your market for a Cajun chicken seasoning mix with the same or similar ingredients. McCormick and Schilling are the two largest producers and there are other brands available.

HARD ROCK CAFE
chili

A HEARTY BEEF-AND-BEAN CHILI SERVED WITH SALTINE CRACKERS.

2 tablespoons vegetable oil

2½ pounds lean beef chuck, coarsely ground for chili

1 large onion, chopped

3 large cloves garlic, crushed

2 tablespoons tomato paste

2 tablespoons Worcestershire sauce

2 tablespoons barbecue sauce, homemade or store-bought

2 tablespoons chili powder

1 tablespoon packed dark brown sugar

1 tablespoon soy sauce

2 teaspoons celery salt

1 teaspoon ground cumin

1 teaspoon black pepper

1 teaspoon seasoned salt

1 teaspoon onion flakes

1 teaspoon granulated garlic

Pinch of cayenne pepper

One 15-ounce can whole tomatoes, chopped, with juice

¾ cup kidney beans, drained and rinsed

One 4-ounce jar pimientos, coarsely chopped, with liquid

1 medium green bell pepper, chopped

¼ cup diced celery

Saltine crackers, for serving

1. Heat the vegetable oil in a large saucepan or Dutch oven and sauté the ground chuck until browned. Drain the fat and add the onion and garlic, and sauté until they are soft. Set aside.

2. Separately, mix together the tomato paste and all the rest of the spices and seasonings, stirring to blend well after each addition.

3. Add the tomato paste mixture to the ground beef mixture and simmer for 5 minutes. Stir in the canned tomatoes with their juice and the drained kidney beans. Reduce the heat to low and cook, covered, for about 15 minutes, stirring occasionally. Add the pimientos, with their liquid, the bell pepper, and the celery, and simmer, uncovered, for about 5 minutes more. Serve in warmed bowls with saltines.

4. The chili can be allowed to cool and refrigerated in a covered container at this point and reheated when ready to serve. It can also be frozen in different-size containers, depending on how many portions you want to serve at one time.

Serves 6 to 8

AT-HOME COST: $9.50

Use any barbecue sauce you prefer or one of the recipes from this book. Seasoned salt from several manufacturers is available at your market—a paprika-based one might also go well with this recipe.

HARD ROCK CAFE

filet steak sandwich

THE CADILLAC OF STEAK SANDWICHES! PERFECTLY GRILLED FILET MIGNON ON A
FRESH SOURDOUGH FRENCH ROLL WITH MAYO AND TANGY MUSTARD.

One 5-ounce filet mignon
Salt and pepper
1 sourdough French roll
1½ tablespoons mayonnaise

1½ tablespoons spicy mustard
½ cup shredded iceberg lettuce
3 tomato slices

1. Light a charcoal grill or preheat the broiler.

2. Slice the filet mignon horizontally into 2 medallions. Grill or broil for
    2 to 4 minutes per side, to your preferred doneness. Season with salt and
    pepper and then cut into ½-inch strips.

3. Split the French roll and dress the top half with the mayonnaise. Spread
    the mustard on the bottom half and layer with the meat strips. Top the
    steak with the shredded lettuce and the tomato slices, then cover with
    the top half of the roll.

4. Cut the sandwich in half on the diagonal and secure each half with a
    toothpick.

Serves 1

AT-HOME COST: $9.50

If this sandwich sounds too bulky, slice the medallions into several
thinner slices after cooking.

HARD ROCK CAFE
grilled-vegetable sandwich

GRILLED BELL PEPPER, SQUASH, AND EGGPLANT TOPPED WITH LETTUCE, TOMATO, ONION, AND MAYONNAISE SERVED ON SOURDOUGH ROLLS.

6 tablespoons mayonnaise
½ teaspoon chopped fresh parsley
Pinch of dried oregano
Salt
1 medium red bell pepper, quartered
1 small zucchini, sliced lengthwise
1 yellow summer squash, sliced lengthwise

¼ eggplant, sliced lengthwise
¼ cup olive oil
2 sourdough French rolls
8 onion ring slices
4 tomato slices
1 tablespoon grated Parmesan cheese
2 large leaves red-leaf lettuce

1. Do ahead: Make the spread with 3 tablespoons of the mayonnaise, the parsley, the oregano, and salt. Blend well and set aside, or refrigerate, covered, until ready to use.

2. Light a charcoal grill or preheat the broiler.

3. Brush the prepared vegetables with the olive oil and grill for 2 to 3 minutes on each side for the bell peppers and 4 to 5 minutes for the squash and eggplant. Turn once and season with salt. When the vegetables begin to char, remove them from the grill, and when cool enough to handle, peel the skin from the bell pepper.

4. Split the French rolls and dress the bottom halves with the mayonnaise spread. First arrange the zucchini, then the yellow squash, then the eggplant, on the bottom halves, and top with the bell pepper. Layer the onion rings and tomato slices over the bell pepper and sprinkle with the Parmesan cheese. Top off the vegetables with the lettuce leaves and spread the top halves of the rolls with the remaining 3 tablespoons mayonnaise. Cover the sandwiches with the top halves of the rolls.

5. Slice the sandwiches in half diagonally and secure the halves with toothpicks.

Serves 2

AT-HOME COST: $5

Vary the vegetable mix by adding or substituting a couple of long, thin strips of carrot.

HARD ROCK CAFE
nice and easy chicken 'n' cheesy

BAKED CHICKEN SERVED OVER SHREDDED CHEESE, TOPPED WITH A CHILI-SPICED CHICKEN BROTH, AND GARNISHED WITH TORTILLA STRIPS.

Two 6-ounce boneless, skinless chicken breasts, cut into ½-inch pieces
1 tablespoon unsalted butter
½ habanero pepper, minced
2 cups pico de gallo, homemade (see page 16 or 70) or store-bought, drained
¼ cup chicken bouillon powder
½ teaspoon paprika
1 tablespoon ground cumin
1 teaspoon chili powder
½ teaspoon garlic salt

For serving
1½ cups shredded Monterey Jack cheese, plus extra for garnish
Chopped fresh cilantro
Tortilla strips
Sour cream, for garnish
Lime wedges, for garnish

1. Do ahead: Preheat the oven to 375°F. Lightly oil a baking sheet and arrange the chicken pieces in a single layer. Bake for about 20 minutes, or until cooked through.

2. Melt the butter in a large stockpot and sauté the habanero pepper and the pico de gallo for 5 minutes, or just until the vegetables are soft. Add 8 cups warm water, the chicken bouillon powder, the spices, and garlic salt. Simmer for about 15 minutes, or until reduced by half. Taste for seasonings—you might like it even hotter!

3. To serve, layer the shredded cheese in the bottom of each soup bowl and add the cooked chicken pieces. Sprinkle with chopped cilantro and tortilla strips. Ladle the broth over the top and garnish with additional shredded cheese and sour cream. Put a lime wedge on the side of the serving plate.

AT-HOME COST: $4.50

Leave out the habanero pepper if you don't want the heat, or add the entire pepper if you like things spicy!

HARD ROCK CAFE
tupelo-style chicken

THIS DISH WAS CREATED BY HARD ROCK CAFE IN HONOR OF ELVIS PRESLEY'S BIRTHPLACE. CRUNCHY CHICKEN FINGERS WITH A NICE ZING SERVED WITH HONEY-MUSTARD AND APRICOT DIPPING SAUCES.

Honey-Mustard Dipping Sauce
¼ cup mayonnaise
1½ teaspoons yellow mustard
2 teaspoons honey
Pinch of paprika

Apricot Dipping Sauce
2 tablespoons Grey Poupon Dijon mustard
1 tablespoon apricot preserves
2 tablespoons honey

1 cup crumbled cornflakes
2 teaspoons red pepper flakes

1¼ teaspoons cayenne pepper
1 teaspoon cumin
1 teaspoon salt
½ teaspoon paprika
¼ teaspoon onion powder
Pinch of garlic powder
4 to 6 cups vegetable oil, for deep-frying
1 cup milk
1 large egg, beaten
1 cup all-purpose flour
1 pound boneless, skinless chicken breasts

1. Do ahead: Make the honey-mustard sauce. Whisk together all the ingredients. Set aside or refrigerate, covered, until ready to use.

2. Do ahead: Make the apricot sauce by whisking all the ingredients together. Set aside or refrigerate, covered, until ready to use.

3. To make the breading, combine the cornflakes with the red pepper flakes, cayenne, cumin, salt, paprika, onion powder, and garlic powder. Whisk until the ingredients are well blended. Set in a shallow dish.

4. Preheat the oil to 350°F in a deep-fryer or a heavy-bottomed saucepan.

5. Beat together the milk and egg, and set in a shallow bowl. Place the flour in a shallow dish.

6. Cut the chicken breasts into ½-inch-wide strips. Coat each strip with the flour and the egg, then coat with the flour again and the egg again.

Press each strip into the cornflake mixture and carefully fry, in batches, for 4 to 5 minutes, until each strip is golden brown and cooked through. Drain on paper towels.

7. Serve with the two dipping sauces in ramekins on the side.

Serves 6 to 8 as an appetizer

AT-HOME COST: $5.50

HOUSTON'S RESTAURANT

canadian cheese soup

A CREAMY, CHEESY SOUP LIGHTLY SPECKLED WITH CARROTS, ONION, AND TOMATOES.

8 tablespoons (1 stick) butter or margarine
1 cup finely diced carrots
½ cup finely diced onion
½ cup finely diced celery
2 to 3 tablespoons all-purpose flour
3 cups half-and-half

3 cups chicken broth
2 pounds Velveeta cheese, cut into cubes

Garnish
1 tablespoon minced fresh parsley
Diced tomatoes
Diced jalapeño pepper

1. In a large saucepan, heat the butter and sauté the carrots, onion, and celery. Do not brown the vegetables; they should just be soft. Whisk in the flour and stir for a minute or two, then add the half-and-half and simmer over low heat. Don't let the mixture boil, just let it simmer until it is thickened.

2. Gradually add the chicken broth, whisking the mixture to combine all the ingredients. The broth should be slightly thickened, like a cream soup. Let it simmer for about 10 minutes so the flour has a chance to cook.

3. Stir in the cheese, whisking constantly, until it is completely melted. Ladle the soup into warmed bowls, garnish with the parsley and, if you like, tomatoes and/or jalapeño.

Serves 4 to 6

AT-HOME COST: $8.50

Drained canned diced tomatoes can be used if fresh tomatoes are not available.

Use a low-sodium chicken broth.

Houston's menu of diverse American classics includes everything from the simplest of appetizers to the most elegant of char-broiled steaks and seafood entrées. Houston's takes pride in using high-quality ingredients, which is why they work closely with area growers and purveyors to ensure that their produce, meat, fish, and chicken are of the highest standard.

HOUSTON'S RESTAURANT

grilled chicken salad

MIXED GREENS AND TORTILLA STRIPS WITH A HONEY-LIME VINAIGRETTE AND PEANUT SAUCE.

Honey-Lime Dressing

½ cup lime juice
4 teaspoons honey mustard
2 cloves garlic, minced
1 teaspoon pepper
½ teaspoon salt
¼ cup plus 3 tablespoons honey

Peanut Sauce

¼ cup soy sauce
¼ cup hot water
¼ cup creamy peanut butter
2 teaspoons Asian sesame oil
1 teaspoon ground ginger

Salad

1 bag mixed salad greens, chilled
1 large carrot, julienned and chilled
2 grilled chicken breasts, cut into
  bite-size pieces and chilled
Thin tortilla strips

1. Do ahead: Make the honey-lime dressing by thoroughly blending all the dressing ingredients. Set aside until ready to use, or refrigerate in a covered container.

2. Do ahead: Make the peanut sauce by thoroughly whisking together all the ingredients. Set aside until ready to use, or refrigerate in a covered container, but bring to room temperature before using.

3. Toss all the salad ingredients with the honey-lime dressing and divide among 4 salad plates. Drizzle with the peanut sauce.

Serves 4

AT-HOME COST: $4.50

HOUSTON'S RESTAURANT

tortilla soup

A HEARTY SOUP OF CHICKEN, VEGETABLES, CHEESE, CORN, AND TOMATOES.

One 2½- to 3-pound chicken, cut up, skin removed
2 ribs celery, cut into chunks
1 medium onion, quartered
1 large carrot, quartered
2 sprigs fresh parsley
2 tablespoons chicken bouillon powder
1 teaspoon lemon pepper
1 large clove garlic, minced
1½ pounds potatoes, peeled
One 14.75-ounce can cream-style corn
One 10-ounce can Ro*Tel tomatoes, crushed, with juice

1½ cups half-and-half
2 to 4 tablespoons minced fresh cilantro
Salt and black pepper
1 cup shredded Cheddar cheese
1 cup shredded Monterey Jack cheese

Garnish
Sour cream
Avocado, cut into chunks
Black olives, pitted and sliced
4 to 6 corn tortillas, cut into ¼-inch strips and fried

1. Place the chicken, celery, onion, carrot, and parsley in a large stockpot. Add enough water to cover by 2 to 3 inches, then add the chicken bouillon powder, lemon pepper, and garlic. Make sure the bouillon powder is well dissolved. Bring the pot to a boil over high heat, then reduce the heat and simmer for about 1 hour, or until the chicken is tender and falling off the bones. Strain the contents of the pot and reserve the broth. Cut the meat into bite-size pieces and discard the bones and vegetables.

2. Boil the potatoes in 4 cups of the reserved chicken broth until they are soft. Remove the pan from the heat and mash the potatoes together with their broth, using a potato masher. Add the creamed corn, tomatoes, half-and-half, and cilantro, mashing and blending well.

3. Heat the potato mixture over low heat and simmer, adding enough of the reserved broth to make a thick and creamy soup, for about 15 minutes. Season to taste with salt and black pepper, then stir in the diced chicken and shredded cheeses.

4. Ladle the soup into warmed bowls and garnish each serving with a dollop of sour cream, chunks of avocado, black olive slices, and the tortilla strips.

Serves 4 to 6

AT-HOME COST: $8.50

Parsley can be substituted for the cilantro in the potato mixture.

Purchase some tortilla chips and gently crumble them to use as a garnish.

HOUSTON'S RESTAURANT

wild rice and mushroom soup

A CREAMY RICE SOUP CHOCK-FULL OF CARROTS, LEEKS, AND MUSHROOMS.

2 cups wild rice
4 tablespoons (½ stick) butter
1¼ cups finely diced carrots
4 ounces leeks, finely diced
1 pound mushrooms, sliced
½ cup all-purpose flour
½ cup sherry
12 cups vegetable broth

4 cups heavy cream
2 tablespoons chopped fresh
thyme, or 2 teaspoons dried
3 tablespoons chopped fresh
parsley, or 1 tablespoon dried,
plus extra for garnish
Salt and pepper

1. Do ahead: Boil the wild rice in 8 cups of water until the grains just start to burst, 30 to 40 minutes. Drain the rice and set aside or refrigerate in a covered container until ready to use.

2. Melt the butter in a stockpot and lightly sauté the carrots and leeks. When they are soft, add the mushrooms and cook until softened. Add the flour to the pot and whisk frequently, until it is lightly colored brown and fully incorporated with the butter.

3. Remove the vegetables from the pot, deglaze the pot with the sherry, scraping up any browned bits, return the vegetables, and add the broth.

4. Simmer for 30 minutes, stirring occasionally. Add the cooked rice and the heavy cream. Continue to simmer until slightly thickened, then add the chopped herbs and season to taste with salt and pepper. Ladle into warmed bowls to serve and garnish with additional parsley, if desired.

Serves 8 to 10

AT-HOME COST: $8.50

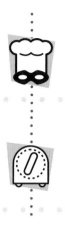

If wild rice is not available, substitute 6 cups cooked brown or white rice.

This dish is a great way to take advantage of leftover cooked rice, couscous, or barley. Pasta lovers can even substitute a small pasta such as orzo.

JACK IN THE BOX

jumbo jack

A JUMBO BEEF PATTY TOPPED WITH LETTUCE, TOMATO, PICKLES, CHOPPED ONION, AND JACK'S SPECIAL SAUCE ON A SESAME SEED BUN.

Special Sauce
1 tablespoon mayonnaise
Dash of lemon juice
Pinch of onion powder
Pinch of sugar
1 teaspoon ketchup

1 sesame seed hamburger bun or plain hamburger bun, split in half

One 4-ounce frozen beef patty
Salt
1 1/2 teaspoons chopped white onion
2 slices dill pickle
2 large lettuce leaves
2 tomato slices

1. Do ahead: Make the special sauce by combining all the ingredients. Set aside, or refrigerate, covered, until ready to use.

2. Light a charcoal grill, or preheat an electric griddle to 400°F.

3. Toast the split hamburger bun on the grill, and set aside. Place the frozen patty on the grill and cook for 4 to 5 minutes per side, salting both sides, turning once, and salting again after turning. Drain before putting on the bun.

4. Spread half the special sauce on the top half of the bun and add the onion, pickle slices, lettuce, and tomato. Spread the remaining sauce on the bottom half of the bun and add the cooked patty. Cover with the top half of the bun and enjoy.

Serves 1

AT-HOME COST: $2.00

Robert O. Peterson started the original Jack in the Box in 1951 with a drive-through restaurant in San Diego. The Jack in the Box menu is extensive and offers burgers—including a sirloin burger—egg rolls, tacos, and a new favorite, the bacon-potato-cheddar wedge. There's something for everybody at Jack's!

JACK IN THE BOX

oreo cookie shake

MADE WITH VANILLA ICE CREAM, OREO COOKIES, WHIPPED CREAM, AND MARASCHINO CHERRIES.

3 cups vanilla ice cream
1½ cups milk
8 Oreo cookies

Whipped cream, for topping
2 maraschino cherries, for garnish

1. Mix the ice cream and milk in a blender and process until smooth.

2. Break up the cookies and add to the ice cream while the blender is running on low. Blend until the cookies are pureed—a few chunks are okay.

3. Pour the mixture into 2 chilled glasses and garnish with whipped cream and a cherry on top.

Serves 2

AT-HOME COST: $3.50

JOE'S CRAB SHACK
harvest bay mahimahi

GRILLED MAHIMAHI TOPPED WITH GARLIC-BUTTERED SAUTÉED SHRIMP AND MUSHROOMS AND TOSSED IN ALFREDO SAUCE.

Garlic Butter
8 tablespoons (1 stick) butter
2 cloves garlic, minced

Four 7-ounce mahimahi fillets
Salt and pepper

½ cup peeled small shrimp
½ cup sliced mushrooms
1 cup Alfredo sauce, homemade
 or store-bought
½ teaspoon minced fresh dill

1. Do ahead: Make the garlic butter. Melt the butter in a small saucepan and add the minced garlic. Simmer over low heat for about 10 minutes. The garlic should be soft and translucent; the butter should not be browned. Let cool, and refrigerate in a covered container until ready to use.

2. Light a charcoal grill or preheat the broiler.

3. Season the mahimahi fillets with salt and pepper and cook, turning once, until the fish is cooked through and flakes easily with a fork, 3 to 5 minutes per side. Set aside and keep warm.

4. Melt the garlic butter in a small skillet and sauté the shrimp and mushrooms (the shrimp will take only a few seconds to cook; the mushrooms should be soft and absorb quite a bit of the melted butter).

5. Whisk in the Alfredo sauce to heat through and blend the flavors; add the dill.

6. Put 1 mahimahi fillet on each warmed plate and spoon the shrimp-and-mushroom sauce over the top. Serve warm.

Serves 4

AT-HOME COST: $6.50

Swordfish, snapper, or albacore tuna can be substituted for the mahimahi.

This restaurant chain was started by two beachgoer buddies in Houston, Texas, in 1991. Joe's Crab Shack now has more than a hundred locations, from California to the East Coast. The restaurants feature a full menu and bar but are well known for their shellfish dishes, such as the Steampot Classic, which features Dungeness crab and Alaska snow crab, and shrimp. As their slogan goes, "Peace, Love and Crabs."

KFC

coleslaw

FRESHLY PREPARED AND DELICIOUS, THIS COLESLAW IS PART OF WHAT MADE THE COLONEL FAMOUS.

Slaw Dressing
¼ cup plus 2½ tablespoons
    vegetable oil
¾ cup minced onion
1 cup sugar

4½ teaspoons tarragon vinegar
2½ cups Miracle Whip

2 carrots, finely chopped
2 heads cabbage, finely shredded

1. Do ahead: Prepare the slaw dressing by combining the vegetable oil, onion, sugar, vinegar, and Miracle Whip, whisking briskly to thoroughly blend all the ingredients. Refrigerate in a covered container until ready to use.

2. Toss together the carrots and cabbage, then fold in the dressing, combining well. Cover and refrigerate overnight. Drain a little of the accumulated liquid before serving.

Serves 8 to 10

AT-HOME COST: $5

KFC—also known as Kentucky Fried Chicken—was begun in 1930 by Harland Sanders in Sanders's Court & Café in Corbin, Kentucky. In 1939 he began using a pressure fryer, which allowed him to serve his customers more quickly. Colonel Sanders created his famous Original Recipe chicken in 1940. KFC is now in more than eighty countries around the world.

KFC
grilled chicken

A HEALTHIER ALTERNATIVE TO KFC ORIGINAL RECIPE CHICKEN, WITH THE SAME SAVORY FLAVOR.

Brine

¼ cup salt

1 tablespoon Accent flavor enhancer

1 2½- to 3-pound chicken, cut into 8 pieces

Dry Rub Seasoning Mix

2 teaspoons all-purpose flour

¼ teaspoon salt

¾ teaspoon chicken bouillon powder

¼ teaspoon beef bouillon powder

¼ teaspoon dried marjoram

¼ teaspoon coarsely ground pepper

¼ teaspoon dried rosemary, crushed

¼ teaspoon dried basil

Pinch of dried oregano

Pinch of garlic powder

¼ cup vegetable oil

¼ teaspoon liquid smoke

¼ teaspoon soy sauce

1. Do ahead: Make the brine. In a pot large enough to hold 8 cups water and all the chicken pieces, dissolve the salt and Accent in the water. Add the chicken pieces, making sure they are submerged. Refrigerate for at least 2 hours. The brining will ensure that the cooked chicken is moist and tender.

2. Do ahead: Combine all the dry rub ingredients and store in a covered container until ready to use.

3. Preheat the oven to 350°F.

4. Combine the vegetable oil, liquid smoke, and soy sauce and set aside.

5. Remove the chicken from the brine and pat dry. Discard the brine. Brush the vegetable oil mixture on both sides of each piece of chicken and then sprinkle generously with the dry rub.

6. Heat a grill or a grill pan with raised ridges, and cook each chicken piece just long enough to make distinctive grill marks on both sides. Transfer

the chicken to a baking sheet and bake in the oven, turning once, until it is golden brown and cooked through, at least 20 minutes on each side.

Serves 4 or 5

AT-HOME COST: $5

The Accent can be replaced with another brand of monosodium glutamate, which can usually be found in the herbs and spices aisle.

You can omit the beef bouillon powder; just increase the total amount of chicken bouillon powder to 1 teaspoon. Instead of a whole chicken, you could also use all legs, all breasts, or all thighs.

LUBY'S CAFETERIA

*baked corned beef brisket
with sour cream new potatoes*

CORNED BEEF ROASTED TO PERFECTION WITH A BROWN SUGAR–MUSTARD
GLAZE, SERVED WITH SOUR CREAM POTATOES THAT HAVE A HINT OF ZING.

4 pounds corned beef brisket
1 cup packed light brown sugar
¼ cup yellow mustard
3 pounds new potatoes, peeled or
   scrubbed

2 cups sour cream
8 tablespoons (1 stick) butter or
   margarine, at room temperature
2 teaspoons prepared horseradish
Salt and white pepper

1. Preheat the oven to 225°F.
2. Wrap the corned beef brisket in heavy-duty foil and seal the edges well.
   Place the brisket in a roasting pan and bake for 3½ hours.
3. Mix the brown sugar and mustard and set aside.
4. Take the brisket out of the oven and increase the temperature to 350°F.
   Unwrap the brisket and spread the brown sugar–mustard mixture all
   over the brisket. Bake, uncovered, for about 15 minutes.
5. While the brisket is baking, cook the potatoes in a pot of boiling water
   until they are tender, 10 to 15 minutes.
6. Drain the potatoes and mix with the sour cream, butter, and horseradish,
   then season with salt and white pepper. Stir gently to coat the potatoes.
7. To serve, thinly slice the brisket against the grain and serve warm with
   the creamy potatoes.

Serves 8

AT-HOME COST: $7

Prepared horseradish is just grated horseradish, vinegar, and salt. Horseradish sauce has several other ingredients in it, and the two types are not always interchangeable.

Luby's Cafeteria is a San Antonio–based chain of cafeteria-style restaurants that has remained successful because of their consistency in serving good food at reasonable prices.

LUBY'S CAFETERIA
fried catfish

LUBY'S SIGNATURE FRIED CATFISH STAYS CRISP ON THE OUTSIDE AND MOIST ON THE INSIDE, EVEN IF YOU HAVE TO KEEP IT WARM IN THE OVEN FOR A SHORT TIME.

¼ cup lemon juice
2 teaspoons Worcestershire sauce
2 cups all-purpose flour
¼ cup paprika
2 tablespoons seasoned salt

Vegetable oil, for frying
Six 7- to 8-ounce catfish fillets
Lemon slices or wedges, for garnish
Fresh parsley sprigs, for garnish

1. Whisk together 2 cups water, the lemon juice, and the Worcestershire sauce in a shallow bowl.

2. In another shallow bowl, combine the flour with the paprika and seasoned salt.

3. In a heavy skillet, heat 1 inch of vegetable oil (or enough to cover the fillets) to 350°F. Dip each fillet first in the lemon juice mixture, then in the flour blend. Shake off any excess flour.

4. Fry the fillets, one at a time, turning once, until the coating is crispy and golden brown. Drain on paper towels.

5. Serve each fillet garnished with lemon and parsley.

Serves 6

AT-HOME COST: $8.50

A good brand of seasoned salt is Lawry's; it's a combination of salt and sugar, with paprika, turmeric, onion powder, and garlic powder. Experiment with a few brands until you find one that suits you.

LUBY'S CAFETERIA
green pea salad

GREEN PEAS, CHEESE, AND RED BELL PEPPER LIGHTLY TOSSED WITH MAYONNAISE AND SERVED CHILLED.

Salad

32 ounces frozen green peas, thawed

I cup finely diced Cheddar cheese

I cup diced celery

½ cup thinly sliced sweet pickle

½ cup diced red bell pepper or pimiento

½ cup mayonnaise

Salt and pepper

Lettuce leaves, for serving

1. Rinse the thawed peas and drain well. Toss with the rest of the salad ingredients and chill for 2 hours.

2. Line salad plates with lettuce leaves, top with the salad, and serve. You could also use supersized martini glasses and call them pea-tinis!

Serves 8

AT-HOME COST: $4.50

Substitute fat-free mayonnaise for regular mayonnaise; substitute a low-fat cheese.

LUBY'S CAFETERIA
mixed-squash casserole

TWO KINDS OF SQUASH WITH CARROTS AND ONION IN A CREAMY SAUCE, COMPLEMENTED BY THE LIGHT CRUNCH OF A CORN BREAD TOPPING.

1 cup julienned carrots
4 cups yellow squash, sliced
1/4 inch thick (3 or 4 medium squash)
4 cups zucchini, sliced 1/4 inch thick (3 or 4 medium zucchini)
1/2 cup chopped onion
One 10.75-ounce can condensed cream of chicken soup

1/2 cup sour cream
1 teaspoon salt
1/2 teaspoon pepper
2/3 cup crumbled corn bread
2/3 cup dry white bread, cut into 1/4-inch pieces
2 tablespoons butter or margarine, melted

1. Bring 4 cups of water to a boil and add the carrots. Two minutes later, add the yellow squash and zucchini. Reduce the heat and simmer until the carrots are crisp-tender. Drain the vegetables and run under cold water to stop the cooking. Set aside until ready to use.

2. Preheat the oven to 350°F.

3. Mix together the onion, cream of chicken soup, and sour cream. Season the mixture with the salt and pepper. Add the blanched vegetables and combine well. Pour into a 2-quart baking dish and cover with foil. Bake for 30 minutes.

4. Separately, combine the crumbled corn bread and the white bread pieces and drizzle the melted butter over the bread, tossing to coat. Take the baking dish out of the oven, remove the foil, and top the casserole with the bread mixture. Return the dish to the oven, uncovered, and bake for about 5 minutes more, or until the bread topping is lightly toasted. Serve warm.

AT-HOME COST: $9.50

Purchase a bag of crumbled corn bread to use in this recipe; check to make sure it is not seasoned.

LUBY'S CAFETERIA
smothered steak with mushroom gravy

A DEFINITE COMFORT FOOD: CUBE STEAK COVERED IN A RICH, THICK, RED WINE–INFUSED MUSHROOM GRAVY.

Steak
¾ cup all-purpose flour
I teaspoon salt
½ teaspoon pepper
Six 5-ounce cube steaks
2 tablespoons vegetable oil

Gravy
2 cups beef broth
One 10.75-ounce can condensed cream of mushroom soup

⅓ cup all-purpose flour
⅓ cup red wine
I tablespoon butter or margarine
I cup thinly sliced mushrooms
2 teaspoons Kitchen Bouquet or other browning and flavoring sauce
Salt and pepper
½ teaspoon minced garlic (optional)

1. To prepare the steak, in a shallow bowl, mix the flour with the salt and pepper. Coat each steak on both sides with the flour and shake off the excess.

2. Heat the oil in a large skillet and fry the steaks, one at a time, turning once, until almost cooked through—there should not be any red juices running out. Set aside.

3. To make the gravy, in a saucepan, combine the beef broth and the cream of mushroom soup and bring to a boil. Separately, mix the flour with ¼ cup of water to make a paste and then whisk the paste into the boiling soup. Reduce the heat and continue to cook, stirring frequently, until the gravy thickens. Add the red wine and continue to simmer.

4. Preheat the oven to 350°F.

5. Melt the butter in a skillet and sauté the sliced mushrooms for 3 to 4 minutes, then add the Kitchen Bouquet. Add the cooked mushrooms to the gravy. Season with salt and pepper and, if you would like a little extra flavor, the minced garlic. Transfer the steaks to a shallow baking

pan large enough to hold all 6 in a single layer. Pour half the gravy over the steaks, then cover the pan with foil. Bake for about 12 minutes, or until desired doneness, then plate the steaks and serve with the remaining mushroom gravy.

Serves 6

AT-HOME COST: $8.50

MACARONI GRILL
carmela's chicken rigatoni

GRILLED CHICKEN, MUSHROOMS, CARAMELIZED ONIONS, FRESH BASIL, AND
PARMESAN CHEESE TOSSED WITH RIGATONI PASTA AND MARSALA CREAM SAUCE.

1 large onion	¾ cup Marsala wine
¼ cup olive oil or vegetable oil	2½ cups heavy cream
2 tablespoons butter	Salt and pepper
8 ounces mushrooms, sliced	1 pound rigatoni pasta, cooked
12 ounces grilled chicken breast,	according to the package
cut into bite-size pieces	directions
2 teaspoons minced fresh basil	Parmesan cheese, for garnish

1. Do ahead: Slice the onion into thin strips and sauté it in 1 tablespoon each of the olive oil and the butter over low heat until the strips are very dark brown and almost mushy. This can't be done in a hurry, so leave yourself plenty of time to let the onion slowly stew.

2. In a large skillet, heat the remaining 1 tablespoon butter and 3 tablespoons oil together and add the mushrooms, chicken pieces, basil, and caramelized onion. Sauté for 1 to 2 minutes. Remove the contents from the pan and set aside.

3. Deglaze the pan with the Marsala and simmer for another minute. Return the chicken mixture to the pan. Add the heavy cream and bring to a boil, then reduce the heat and simmer until the sauce is slightly thickened. Season with salt and pepper.

4. Add the cooked rigatoni to the Marsala cream sauce and combine well to blend all the ingredients. Garnish with Parmesan cheese and serve in warmed bowls.

Serves 4

AT-HOME COST: $8.50

Substitute cooked pork or cooked Italian sausage for the grilled chicken.

This is a great way to use leftover cooked chicken.

MACARONI GRILL
chicken scaloppine

SAUTÉED CHICKEN WITH MUSHROOMS, ARTICHOKES, CAPERS, AND IMPORTED PROSCIUTTO IN A LEMON-BUTTER SAUCE. SERVED OVER CAPELLINI PASTA.

Lemon-Butter Sauce
1/2 cup lemon juice
1/4 cup white wine
1/2 cup heavy cream
I pound (4 sticks) butter, cut into pieces
Salt and pepper

Six to eight 3-ounce boneless, skinless chicken breasts, pounded thin
Salt and pepper

2¾ cups all-purpose flour
Butter, for sautéing
Oil, for sautéing
6 ounces prosciutto, diced
12 ounces mushrooms, sliced
12 ounces artichoke hearts, sliced
I tablespoon drained capers
I pound capellini (angel hair) pasta, cooked according to the package directions
Chopped fresh parsley, for garnish

1. Do ahead: Make the lemon-butter sauce: In a small saucepan, combine the lemon juice and white wine and reduce by one-third over medium heat. Whisk in the heavy cream and let the mixture thicken, 3 to 4 minutes. Reduce the heat and add the pieces of butter, one by one, constantly whisking, until each piece is fully incorporated. Season with salt and pepper. Remove from the heat and set aside. This can be refrigerated, but it must be gently reheated by whisking over low heat.

2. Season the chicken breasts with salt and pepper and dredge each side with the flour. Heat butter and oil in a skillet large enough to hold the chicken, and sauté the breasts until cooked through, and no longer pink in the middle, turning once. If your skillet is not large enough, cook the breasts in batches. Remove the cooked chicken and keep warm.

3. Add the prosciutto, mushrooms, artichoke hearts, and capers to the skillet and sauté until the mushrooms are soft. Add half of the lemon-butter sauce to the skillet and gently simmer to coat the vegetables, 1 to 2 minutes.

4. Return the chicken to the pan and turn to coat both sides with the sauce. Plate the cooked pasta and cover each serving with the remaining lemon-butter sauce. Put 1 chicken breast on top of each portion of pasta and pour the pan sauce over the chicken. Garnish with chopped parsley.

Serves 6 to 8

AT-HOME COST: $9.50

Substitute spaghetti or vermicelli for the capellini. Pancetta can be substituted for prosciutto. Artichoke hearts come frozen, canned, or marinated. If using marinated ones, be sure to rinse off the marinade before adding them.

MACARONI GRILL

farfalle di pollo al sugo bianco

BOW-TIE PASTA WITH CHICKEN AND PANCETTA, TOSSED IN A CREAMY ASIAGO CHEESE SAUCE.

Asiago Sauce
2 cups heavy cream
¼ teaspoon chicken bouillon
  powder
1¼ cups shredded Asiago cheese
1 tablespoon cornstarch

Pasta
4 tablespoons (½ stick) butter
½ cup diced red onion
½ cup chopped pancetta

1 tablespoon chopped garlic
¾ cup chopped green onions
  (green parts only)
12 ounces grilled chicken, sliced
1 pound farfalle (bow-tie) pasta,
  cooked according to the package
  directions
½ cup heavy cream
1 tablespoon chopped fresh
  parsley, for garnish

1. Do ahead: Make the Asiago sauce. In a medium saucepan, heat the heavy cream until it just starts to bubble, then whisk in the chicken bouillon powder and the shredded cheese. Blend ¼ cup water and the cornstarch and whisk into the cream sauce. Let the mixture thicken, then remove from the heat and set aside, or let cool and refrigerate, covered, until ready to use. Bring the sauce back up to temperature very carefully, whisking frequently, until it just simmers for about 1 minute.

2. In a large skillet, melt the butter and sauté the red onion, pancetta, and garlic. Let simmer until the vegetables are just softened. Add the green onions, grilled chicken, and the cooked pasta. Add the heavy cream to the pan, then add the Asiago sauce. Stir frequently to blend all the ingredients.

3. Pour the creamy pasta into warmed bowls and garnish with the chopped parsley.

Serves 4

AT-HOME COST: $9.50

Substitute 4 ounces of regular bacon if you can't find pancetta; dice it and cook it partially before adding to the pasta sauce.

Romano's Macaroni Grill bills itself as a chain of casual Italian dining restaurants located around the world. The first Romano's Macaroni Grill was opened in San Antonio, Texas, in 1988 by Phil Romano. The chain is known for great Italian dishes. And have fun with the paper tablecloths and crayons!

MACARONI GRILL

fondata gamberi

SHRIMP IN A CREAMY, CHEESY DIPPING SAUCE WITH ARTICHOKES AND SPINACH,
PERFECTLY SEASONED. FOR AN ENTRÉE, TRY IT WITH YOUR FAVORITE PASTA!

3 tablespoons butter
1 shallot, minced
2 tablespoons all-purpose flour
2 cups half-and-half
1 tablespoon clam juice
2 tablespoons dry white wine
4 cups coarsely chopped spinach
1 cup chopped artichoke hearts

8 large shrimp, peeled, deveined,
  and diced
Pinch of cayenne pepper
Salt and black pepper
½ cup shredded mozzarella cheese

For Serving
Garlic-cheese bread or grilled
  toast points

1. In a medium saucepan, melt the butter and sauté the shallot until it is translucent. Whisk in the flour to make a smooth paste. Gradually add the half-and-half, clam juice, and white wine. Let the mixture simmer for a few minutes, until it has thickened. Stir frequently to keep the sauce smooth.

2. Add the chopped spinach, artichokes, and shrimp. Season with the cayenne, salt, and black pepper. Use a little extra cayenne if you like a little heat! Whisk in the mozzarella and stir until it is melted and smooth.

3. Pour into a warmed bowl and serve with garlic-cheese bread or grilled toast points.

Serves 6 to 8 as an appetizer

AT-HOME COST: $9

Artichoke hearts come frozen, canned, or marinated. If using marinated ones, be sure to rinse off the marinade before adding them.

MACARONI GRILL

polpettone alla montagona (italian meat loaf)

MILDLY FLAVORED MEAT LOAF STUDDED WITH ONION AND MUSHROOMS—TOPPED WITH YOUR CHOICE OF MELTED CHEESE.

2 cups dry bread crumbs
2 cups milk
2½ pounds ground beef
1 teaspoon salt
½ teaspoon pepper
1 medium onion, diced

1 cup sliced button mushrooms
6 fresh sage leaves, minced
½ cup ketchup
2 large eggs
Sliced cheese

1. Do ahead: Soak the bread crumbs in the milk for about 15 minutes, or until all the milk has been absorbed.

2. Using the paddle attachment of a stand mixer, blend the ground beef with the salt, pepper, onion, mushrooms, sage, ketchup, and eggs on low speed for about 4 minutes. Add the softened bread crumbs and mix for another 4 to 5 minutes.

3. Preheat the oven to 350°F. Grease 1 large or 2 smaller loaf pans.

4. Fill the prepared loaf pan(s) with the ground beef mixture. Tap firmly on a solid surface to settle the mixture and release air bubbles. Cover with foil and poke holes for steam to escape.

5. Bake for 1 hour, or until a thermometer inserted into the middle of the loaf reaches 165°F. Drain any accumulated liquid. Let the loaf stand for 15 minutes, then carefully invert the pan onto a plate—the loaf should easily come out.

6. To serve, preheat the broiler and cover a slice of meat loaf with cheese. Broil for a few minutes, until the cheese is melted.

AT-HOME COST: $9

Substitute ground turkey or chicken for the ground beef. Use cooking spray to prepare the loaf pans.

MACARONI GRILL

shrimp portofino

JUMBO SHRIMP SAUTÉED WITH FRESH SPINACH, MUSHROOMS, AND PINE NUTS, TOPPED WITH A LEMON-BUTTER SAUCE, AND SERVED WITH CAPELLINI PASTA.

1 tablespoon pine nuts

Lemon-Butter Sauce
16 tablespoons (2 sticks) butter, cut into pieces
1½ teaspoons minced shallot
1½ teaspoons minced garlic
¼ cup lemon juice
¼ cup dry white wine
½ cup heavy cream
Salt
Pinch of white pepper

Sautéed Shrimp
2 tablespoons butter
1 to 4 tablespoons minced garlic
1½ cups mushrooms, sliced ¼ inch thick
12 jumbo shrimp, peeled and deveined
3 cups spinach (leaves only)

1 pound capellini (angel hair) pasta, cooked according to the package directions

1. Do ahead: Toast the pine nuts. Heat a large dry frying pan over medium-high heat. Add the whole nuts and toast, stirring often. When the nuts are fragrant with a light-brown color, remove them from the heat. This should take only a couple of minutes. Let the pine nuts cool on a plate or paper towels before using.

2. Make the lemon-butter sauce in a medium saucepan. Melt 2 tablespoons of the butter and sauté the shallot and garlic until they are translucent and soft—do not let the vegetables or the butter get brown. Add the lemon juice and white wine and reduce by half, then add the heavy cream and reduce again by half. Season with salt and white pepper, then add the remaining 14 tablespoons (1¾ sticks) butter, whisking it in, piece by piece, over very low heat.

3. To cook the shrimp, melt the 2 tablespoons butter in a large skillet and sauté the garlic until soft. Add the mushrooms, sauté for a minute or two, then add the shrimp; cook until they are pink.

4. Add the spinach by gently folding it in (it just needs to be wilted, not cooked all the way through). Add the toasted pine nuts.

5. To serve, place the pasta on warmed plates with the shrimp mixture on the side. Pour the lemon-butter sauce over the pasta, and drizzle a little over the shrimp.

Serves 4

AT-HOME COST: $9

MRS. FIELDS
applesauce-oatmeal cookies

OATMEAL DROP COOKIES STUDDED WITH FRESH APPLE PIECES AND RAISINS,
WITH JUST THE RIGHT BLEND OF SPICES, THEN SWEETENED WITH APPLESAUCE
AND HONEY.

2½ cups all-purpose flour
1 cup quick-cooking rolled oats
½ teaspoon salt
1 teaspoon baking soda
1 teaspoon ground cinnamon
¼ teaspoon ground cloves
2 teaspoons grated lemon zest
1 cup packed dark brown sugar
12 tablespoons (1½ sticks)
    unsalted butter, softened

1 large egg
½ cup unsweetened applesauce
½ cup honey
1 cup finely chopped peeled apple
1 cup raisins
½ cup quick-cooking rolled oats
    (optional)

1. Preheat the oven to 300°F.

2. In a large bowl, combine the flour, the 1 cup rolled oats, salt, baking soda, cinnamon, cloves, and lemon zest. Whisk everything together so that all the dry ingredients are evenly distributed.

3. In another large bowl, beat the brown sugar and butter until the mixture is light and fluffy. With the mixer running, add the egg, then the applesauce, then the honey.

4. Gradually add the dry ingredients, 1 cup at a time, mixing well after each addition; then add the chopped apple and raisins and mix until they are just combined.

5. Drop by rounded tablespoonfuls, about 1½ inches apart, onto ungreased baking sheets. Sprinkle with the ½ cup rolled oats, if desired. Bake for 20 to 25 minutes, until the bottoms are golden. Transfer to wire racks to cool.

AT-HOME COST: $4.50

In 1977, Debbie Fields began selling her homemade cookies, brownies, pretzels, and other baked goods, as well as ice cream and candies. Her goodies have since become an international favorite, being sold in South America, Europe, Asia, and Australia, as well as throughout North America.

MRS. FIELDS
pumpkin harvest cookies

A FALL FAVORITE! PUMPKIN COOKIES WITH CHUNKS OF WHITE CHOCOLATE AND TOASTED PECANS, FRESHLY BAKED.

1 cup pecan halves and pieces
2¼ cups all-purpose flour
1 teaspoon pumpkin pie spice
½ teaspoon baking soda
1½ cups packed dark brown sugar
½ pound (2 sticks) unsalted butter, softened

1 cup pumpkin puree
1 tablespoon vanilla extract
2 large eggs
10 ounces white chocolate, coarsely chopped

1. Preheat the oven to 300°F.

2. Do ahead: Toast the pecans. Spread the nuts out on a baking sheet and bake just until they begin to color, stirring often. Set aside to cool.

3. In a bowl, combine the flour, pumpkin pie spice, and baking soda.

4. In a large bowl, beat the brown sugar and butter until light and fluffy. Gradually beat in the pumpkin puree, vanilla extract, and the eggs, one at a time. Add the dry ingredients, one cup at a time, until just combined—do not overmix. Stir in the chocolate and pecans.

5. Drop by rounded tablespoonfuls, about 2 inches apart, onto ungreased baking sheets. Bake for 20 to 25 minutes, then transfer to wire racks to cool.

Makes 48 cookies

AT-HOME COST: $6.50

O'CHARLEY'S
potato soup

AN OLD-FASHIONED, CREAMY POTATO-AND-CHEESE SOUP, TOPPED WITH BACON, CHIVES, AND SHREDDED CHEDDAR CHEESE.

8 ounces bacon
3 pounds red potatoes, scrubbed
4 tablespoons (½ stick) butter
½ cup all-purpose flour
4 cups half-and-half
I cup milk
I cup chicken stock
I pound Velveeta cheese, melted

White pepper
Garlic powder
I teaspoon Tabasco sauce

Garnish
I cup shredded Cheddar cheese
½ cup snipped fresh chives
½ cup chopped fresh parsley

1. Do ahead: Dice the bacon and cook in a skillet until all the fat is rendered. Drain the bacon and set aside until ready to use.

2. Do ahead: Cut the potatoes into ½-inch dice and put them in a pot with water to cover. Boil for 10 minutes, drain, and set aside.

3. Melt the butter in a heavy pot and add the flour, whisking constantly until the paste is smooth. Gradually add the half-and-half, milk, and chicken stock, whisking constantly. When the sauce begins to thicken, add the Velveeta, whisking frequently.

4. Add the potatoes to the cheese mixture. Season to taste with white pepper and garlic powder, and add the Tabasco. Lower the heat and simmer, covered, for 30 minutes, stirring occasionally.

5. Ladle the soup into warmed bowls and garnish with the bacon bits, shredded Cheddar, chives, and parsley.

AT-HOME COST: $9.50

With more than 230 restaurants in twenty states, this chain offers a moderately priced menu that features steak, chicken, pasta, and seafood.

THE OLD SPAGHETTI FACTORY

spaghetti with browned butter and mizithra cheese

A SIMPLE ITALIAN FAVORITE WITH A DELICIOUS GREEK CHEESE.

½ pound (2 sticks) butter
12 ounces spaghetti, cooked according to the package directions

1 cup shredded Mizithra cheese (see Note)
Salt and pepper

1. Melt the butter in a small saucepan over medium heat and bring it to an easy boil. The solids, which will initially appear as the foam on top, will sink to the bottom of the saucepan and begin to brown. The boiling evaporates the water, so you are left with the toasted solids and the butter oil. This should take 5 to 10 minutes. Remove from the heat and set aside.

2. To serve, toss the hot pasta with the browned butter and the Mizithra cheese. Season with salt and pepper.

Note: Mizithra cheese is a Greek goat-sheep cheese that is similar in taste, texture, and consistency to Italian ricotta salata.

Serves 4

AT-HOME COST: $5

Started in Portland, Oregon, in 1969, in 2008 The Old Spaghetti Factory was recognized by *Parents* magazine as one of the top ten kid-friendly restaurant chains in the country. It offers a large selection of authentic Italian dishes.

OLIVE GARDEN
cheese ravioli with vegetables

CHEESE-FILLED RAVIOLI TOSSED IN A CHICKEN-BASED SAUCE WITH ROASTED
RED PEPPERS, SUN-DRIED TOMATOES, ZUCCHINI, AND OLIVES.

¼ cup extra virgin olive oil
1 clove garlic, chopped
One 7-ounce jar roasted red
  peppers, drained and sliced into
  strips
½ cup julienned oil-packed
  sun-dried tomatoes
½ cup sliced pitted black olives
1 medium zucchini, diced

1 cup chicken broth
Salt
Coarsely ground black pepper
1 pound cheese ravioli, cooked
  according to the package
  directions
Grated Parmesan or Romano
  cheese, for garnish
Chopped fresh parsley, for garnish

1. In a large saucepan, heat the olive oil and sauté the garlic with the
   roasted red peppers, sun-dried tomatoes, olives, and zucchini. When the
   zucchini is crisp-tender, add the chicken broth and season with salt and
   pepper. Simmer for 2 minutes.

2. Add the cooked ravioli to the sauce and simmer for a few minutes to
   heat through, tossing the ravioli gently to coat them with the sauce.

3. Transfer to a warmed serving platter and garnish with grated cheese and
   parsley.

Serves 4

AT-HOME COST: $9

Add marinated artichokes to this dish, if desired.

Founded in 1982, Olive Garden restaurants offer Tuscan-style cuisine as well as their award-winning Tuscan wines to their customers. In 1999, the chain established the Olive Garden Culinary Institute of Tuscany, which teaches chefs how to prepare authentic Italian dishes.

OLIVE GARDEN
chicken scampi

TENDER PIECES OF CHICKEN SAUTÉED WITH BELL PEPPER, ROASTED GARLIC, AND ONION IN A CREAMY GARLIC SAUCE OVER ANGEL HAIR PASTA.

10 cloves garlic, peeled
Olive oil

White Sauce
1 tablespoon butter
2 tablespoons all-purpose flour
¾ cup hot milk

Scampi Sauce Base
3 tablespoons butter
2 tablespoons crushed garlic
2 tablespoons prepared Italian seasoning blend

Black pepper
¾ teaspoon red pepper flakes
¾ cup white wine
1 cup chicken broth

2 boneless, skinless chicken breasts, sliced
1 red bell pepper, julienned
1 red onion, thinly sliced
8 ounces angel hair pasta, cooked according to the package directions

1. Preheat the oven to 400°F.
2. Do ahead: In a small ovenproof saucepan, sauté the garlic cloves in a small amount of olive oil. Put the pan in the oven for 20 to 30 minutes, or cover and slowly roast on the stovetop over low heat. Either way, make sure the garlic doesn't burn, as it will taste bitter. Reserve the oil used for roasting.
3. Make the white sauce: In a small saucepan, melt the 1 tablespoon butter and whisk in the flour, stirring constantly until the paste is smooth. Gradually add the hot milk, whisking continually. Simmer until the sauce is thickened. Set aside.
4. Make the scampi sauce base: In another saucepan, heat the 3 tablespoons butter and add the crushed garlic, the Italian seasoning blend, the black pepper, and red pepper flakes. Cook for about 2 minutes over low heat, then add the wine and chicken broth. Simmer for about 30 minutes.
5. Add ¼ cup of the white sauce to the scampi sauce base and whisk to combine all the ingredients. Simmer until the liquid has thickened.

6. Heat the reserved olive oil in a large saucepan and sauté the chicken until it is almost cooked through. Add the bell pepper and red onion and continue to sauté. When the chicken is cooked through and no longer pink in the middle, add the scampi sauce. Simmer until everything is warmed and then add the roasted garlic cloves. Plate the pasta in warmed bowls and pour the chicken, vegetables, and sauce over the top.

Serves 2

AT-HOME COST: $8

OLIVE GARDEN

clams bruschetta

A TRADITIONAL BRUSCHETTA OF THICK-SLICED, TOASTED BREAD WITH A TOPPING OF FRESH TOMATOES, CLAM MEAT, AND BASIL DRIZZLED WITH EXTRA VIRGIN OLIVE OIL.

8 thick, diagonally cut slices Italian or French bread
1 clove garlic, cut in half
4 large tomatoes, cut into 8 thick slices
1 cup chopped canned clam meat, drained
Kosher salt
Black pepper
½ cup extra virgin olive oil
12 fresh basil leaves, shredded

1. Preheat the grill or broiler.
2. Toast the slices of bread on both sides. Rub with the cut side of the garlic.
3. Place 1 tomato slice and 2 tablespoons of clam meat on each slice of toasted bread and arrange the slices on a warmed serving platter. Sprinkle with salt and a few grinds of black pepper. Drizzle with the olive oil and top with the fresh basil. Serve warm.

Serves 4

AT-HOME COST: $6.50

If ripe tomatoes are not available, you can use diced canned tomatoes.

You can also use cooked shrimp or crabmeat in place of the clams.

OLIVE GARDEN
gnocchi with spicy tomato and wine sauce

A SPICY TOMATO AND WINE SAUCE MAKES THESE POTATO DUMPLINGS REALLY SPECIAL.

¼ cup extra virgin olive oil
12 cloves garlic, peeled
¼ teaspoon red pepper flakes
1 tablespoon chopped fresh basil, or 1 teaspoon dried, plus extra for garnish
1 teaspoon chopped fresh marjoram
2 cups dry white wine
2 cups chicken broth
Two 28-ounce cans whole tomatoes, diced tomatoes, or crushed tomatoes, with juice

8 tablespoons (1 stick) butter, chilled, cut into pieces
½ cup grated Parmesan cheese, plus extra for garnish
Salt and black pepper
4 pounds gnocchi, fresh or frozen, cooked according to the package directions

1. Heat the olive oil in a large saucepan and sauté the garlic, red pepper flakes, the 1 tablespoon fresh basil, and the marjoram until the garlic is a light golden brown. Add the white wine and chicken broth and simmer for about 10 minutes. When the liquid is reduced by half, add the tomatoes and simmer for another 30 minutes.

2. When the sauce is reduced, put half of it into a blender and puree with the butter and the ½ cup Parmesan cheese. Season with salt and black pepper.

3. Return the pureed sauce to the saucepan with the chunky tomato mixture and stir to combine.

4. Put the warm gnocchi in a serving bowl and cover with the sauce. Garnish with Parmesan and basil.

Serves 8 to 12

AT-HOME COST: $9.50

Add some heavy cream to the pureed sauce to make it a little richer.

This sauce would work equally well with other pastas, such as penne, farfalle, and rigatoni. You could also add vegetables and chicken for a filling meal.

OLIVE GARDEN

golden cinnamon orzo calabrese

A TRADITIONAL DESSERT OF ORZO, GOLDEN RAISINS, WALNUTS, AND APPLE
BUTTER.

¼ cup walnut halves

8 ounces orzo pasta, cooked
according to the package
directions

One 12-ounce can evaporated
milk or evaporated skim milk

3 tablespoons sugar

1 tablespoon ground cinnamon

½ cup golden raisins or dark
raisins

¼ cup prepared apple butter

1. Do ahead: Put the walnuts in a small ovenproof skillet and toast in a
   preheated 400°F oven. Bake, tossing often, until the nuts are a light
   golden brown. (Or toast in a dry skillet over low heat, tossing often.)
   Let cool, then chop.

2. Put the cooked orzo into a pot and add the evaporated milk, sugar, and
   cinnamon. Simmer until the liquid is mostly absorbed, then remove
   from the heat.

3. Stir in the raisins, chopped walnuts, and apple butter. When the ingredients are combined, pour the mixture into small bowls and let it set for
   10 minutes. To serve it cold, cover and refrigerate.

Serves 4

AT-HOME COST: $5

Plum-apple butter or pumpkin-apple butter can be substituted for
plain apple butter.

For an artful presentation, invert the chilled dessert on a plate and carefully lift off the bowl. Sprinkle the mound with a little cinnamon-sugar mixture (use the ratio on opposite page) and garnish with mint sprigs.

OLIVE GARDEN
italian pasta salad supremo with primavera toast

A SALAD LOADED WITH ROTINI PASTA, BELL PEPPER, FRESH TOMATO, SALAMI, CAPOCOLLO, ROASTED RED PEPPERS, AND SUN-DRIED TOMATOES IN A BALSAMIC VINAIGRETTE, TOPPED WITH PARMESAN AND ROMANO CHEESES.

Pasta Salad
6 ounces tricolor rotini pasta, cooked according to the package directions
½ cup diced green bell pepper
½ cup diced red bell pepper
1 beefsteak tomato, diced
1½ teaspoons chopped garlic
3 tablespoons julienned oil-packed sun-dried tomatoes
¼ cup chopped fresh basil
4 ounces Genoa salami, julienned
4 ounces capocollo ham, julienned
4 ounces pepperoni, sliced
¼ cup sliced roasted red peppers
4 ounces Provolone cheese, diced

Vinaigrette
3 tablespoons grated Parmesan cheese
3 tablespoons grated Romano cheese
½ cup extra virgin olive oil
½ cup balsamic vinegar
Salt and pepper

Primavera Toast
½ loaf Italian or French bread, sliced diagonally
1 cup mayonnaise
½ green onion, minced
1½ teaspoons chopped garlic
¼ cup grated Parmesan and Romano cheeses
Paprika

Garnish
Lettuce leaves or spring mix of greens
Paprika
Basil leaves
Grated Parmesan and Romano cheeses
Grape tomatoes

1. In a large mixing bowl, toss all the pasta salad ingredients together and refrigerate, covered, until ready to use. In a small bowl, combine all the vinaigrette ingredients and set aside.

2. Preheat the oven to 350°F.

3. Prepare the toast by toasting the slices of bread on only one side.

4. Combine the mayonnaise, green onion, and garlic, mixing well. Spread on the untoasted side of the bread and sprinkle with the ¼ cup grated cheese and paprika. Put the slices on a baking sheet and return to the oven for 6 to 8 minutes, until the cheese is melted and the topping is light brown.

5. To serve, lay a lettuce leaf down on a chilled salad plate and mound 1 cup of the salad in the center. Drizzle with the vinaigrette. Garnish with the paprika, basil leaves, grated cheese, and grape tomatoes. Put the toast on the side of the plate.

Serves 6

AT-HOME COST: $9.75

Capocollo is a dry-cured boneless pork shoulder butt that can be enjoyed in salads or sandwiches.

OLIVE GARDEN
italian sausage soup

TUSCAN-STYLE ITALIAN SAUSAGE SOUP WITH RICE AND SPINACH.

1 pound bulk sweet Italian sausage
1 cup converted white rice
6 cups beef broth
1 cup chopped tomatoes
2 tablespoons tomato paste

Salt and pepper
One 10-ounce box frozen spinach,
   thawed, drained, and chopped
Grated Pecorino Romano cheese,
   for garnish

1. Sauté the sausage in a stockpot, breaking it up as it cooks. When thoroughly browned, add the rice and stir until it is completely coated in the fat from the sausage. Add the beef broth, tomatoes, tomato paste, salt, and ¼ teaspoon pepper and bring to a boil.

2. Reduce the heat and simmer for 12 to 15 minutes, until the rice is tender. Add the chopped spinach, but make sure it is well drained; squeeze it in a dish towel if necessary to get the moisture out. Let the soup simmer for a few minutes, then season with salt and pepper.

3. Ladle the soup into warmed bowls and garnish with the grated cheese.

Serves 4

AT-HOME COST: $9

OLIVE GARDEN

italian sausage–stuffed portobello mushrooms with an herb and parmesan cheese sauce

ITALIAN SAUSAGE, GARLIC CROUTONS, AND AN ITALIAN BLEND OF HERBS BAKED IN MUSHROOM CAPS AND TOPPED WITH A CREAMY PARMESAN-BASIL SAUCE.

Cream Sauce

2 cups heavy cream

¼ cup grated Parmesan cheese

2 tablespoons chopped fresh basil, or 2 teaspoons dried

Salt and pepper

Stuffing

2 large eggs

¼ cup milk

1 teaspoon chopped fresh Italian flat-leaf parsley

1 teaspoon chopped fresh basil

1 teaspoon chopped fresh marjoram

1 clove garlic, chopped

1 cup finely ground garlic croutons

¼ cup grated Parmesan cheese

1 pound bulk Italian sausage

4 large portobello mushrooms

Fresh parsley sprigs or basil leaves, for garnish

1. Do ahead: Make the cream sauce. Bring the heavy cream to a gentle boil and reduce by half. Add the ¼ cup Parmesan cheese, basil, and salt and pepper. Set aside.

2. Do ahead: Prepare the stuffing. Whisk the eggs in a large bowl, then add the milk and combine well. Add the parsley, basil, marjoram, garlic, ground croutons, and ¼ cup Parmesan cheese. Set aside. Sauté the sausage in a skillet, breaking it up as it cooks. When it is thoroughly browned, remove it with a slotted spoon and add it to the stuffing mixture, stirring well to combine.

3. Preheat the oven to 350°F.

4. Remove the stems and the spongy undersides of the mushrooms so that they resemble hollowed-out bowls. Place them, open side down, on a baking sheet and bake for about 8 minutes, or until they are a little soft.

5. Stuff the mushroom caps with the sausage mixture and put them back in the oven to bake for 15 to 20 minutes, until they are golden brown on top and cooked through.

6. To serve, spoon a little of the cream sauce over each mushroom and garnish with a sprig of parsley or fresh basil. Serve warm.

Serves 4

AT-HOME COST: $9.50

OLIVE GARDEN
pasta frittata

A TYPICAL ITALIAN FRITTATA, WITH PASTA AND BACON.

4 ounces thick-cut bacon, diced
Cooking spray or margarine

Frittata Batter
4 extra-large eggs or 5 large eggs, beaten
2½ cups half-and-half
5 teaspoons cornstarch
Salt and white pepper
Pinch of nutmeg (optional)

12 ounces spaghetti, broken into 2-inch pieces, cooked according to the package directions
¼ cup sliced green onions
¼ teaspoon white pepper
Heaped ¼ cup shredded Fontina cheese
Grated Parmesan cheese

1. Do ahead: Sauté the diced bacon until it is cooked through. Drain on paper towels and set aside.

2. Preheat the oven to 350°F. Spray a 1½-quart baking dish with the cooking spray and set aside.

3. To make the frittata batter, beat together the eggs, half-and-half, and cornstarch with salt and white pepper and the nutmeg, if desired. Make sure the eggs have been thoroughly beaten and incorporated with the half-and-half.

4. Combine the cooked spaghetti with the green onions, bacon bits, and white pepper. Mix well and transfer to the prepared baking dish. Pour the frittata batter over the spaghetti and bake for 25 minutes, or until the center is firm.

5. Sprinkle with the Fontina cheese and return to the oven and bake until the cheese is golden. Turn off the heat and open the door to let the frittata dry out a little. This will make it firm enough to slice.

6. Sprinkle with Parmesan cheese and serve on warmed plates.

AT-HOME COST: $6.50

Use egg substitute for the whole eggs; use whole wheat pasta.

OLIVE GARDEN

penne senese

PENNE PASTA TOSSED IN A HEARTY CREAM SAUCE OF SAUSAGE, PROSCIUTTO, ONION, MUSHROOMS, AND GARLIC—FLAVORED WITH ITALIAN HERBS AND TOPPED WITH FRESHLY GRATED PECORINO ROMANO CHEESE.

½ cup chopped onion

3 cloves garlic, chopped

2 tablespoons butter

½ cup extra virgin olive oil

8 ounces portobello or button mushrooms, sliced

6 Italian sausage links, casings removed

¼ cup plus 2 tablespoons white wine or chicken broth

2 tablespoons all-purpose flour

4 cups heavy cream or half-and-half

4 ounces prosciutto, chopped

1 tablespoon minced fresh sage, or 1 teaspoon dried, plus extra for garnish

1 tablespoon minced fresh parsley, or 1 teaspoon parsley flakes

8 ounces Pecorino Romano cheese, grated, plus extra for garnish

1 teaspoon garlic powder

Salt and white pepper

1 pound penne pasta, cooked according to the package directions

1. Sauté the onion and garlic in a mixture of the butter and olive oil. Add the mushrooms and sauté for a few minutes, then add the sausage, breaking it up as it cooks. When the sausage is no longer pink, add the wine and bring it to a boil. Gradually add the flour, whisking constantly, then stir in the heavy cream, prosciutto, fresh herbs, Pecorino Romano cheese, garlic powder, and salt and white pepper until the sauce is thickened and smooth.

2. Simmer the thickened sauce for about 10 minutes over low heat, stirring frequently.

3. Toss the sauce with the cooked pasta and transfer to a warmed serving platter. Garnish with the extra fresh herbs and grated cheese.

Serves 4

AT-HOME COST: $9

OLIVE GARDEN
risotto milanese

A CREAMY RISOTTO WITH ONION, MUSHROOMS, AND PARMESAN CHEESE.

¼ cup olive oil
½ cup finely chopped onion
½ teaspoon ground turmeric
½ cup sliced mushrooms
5 cups chicken or vegetable
  broth
1 ½ cups Arborio rice

½ cup white wine
½ cup grated Parmesan
  cheese
2 tablespoons butter
Salt and pepper
Fresh parsley sprigs, for
  garnish

1. Heat the olive oil in a stockpot over medium heat and sauté the onion and turmeric until the onion is soft. Add the mushrooms and sauté until they absorb some of the liquid.

2. Heat the broth in a saucepan and keep warm.

3. Add the rice to the sautéed vegetables and stir until all the grains are coated with the olive oil mixture. Add the white wine and let it evaporate, stirring frequently.

4. Add the warm broth, ½ cup at a time, allowing it to be absorbed after each addition, stirring constantly. Repeat this procedure until all the broth is absorbed and the rice is al dente.

5. Remove the pan from the heat and add the Parmesan cheese and the butter, mixing gently after each addition. Season with salt and pepper. Transfer to a warmed serving bowl and garnish with parsley.

Serves 4

AT-HOME COST: $6

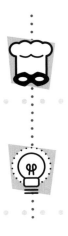

Substitute additional broth for white wine.

Finished risotto is creamy; rice is firm.

OLIVE GARDEN
shrimp cristoforo

SHRIMP SAUTÉED IN A BASIL-BUTTER SAUCE SERVED OVER LINGUINE PASTA.

2½ sticks butter, softened
1 teaspoon minced garlic
Salt and pepper
Heaped ½ cup grated Pecorino
  Romano cheese, plus extra for
  serving
¼ cup fresh basil leaves, chopped
  in a food processer

1 pound medium shrimp, peeled
  and deveined
1 pound linguine pasta, cooked
  according to the package
  directions

1. Do ahead: Use a hand mixer to beat the butter, garlic, and salt and pepper until smooth and creamy. Add the Pecorino Romano cheese and the chopped basil. Cover and refrigerate until ready to use.

2. Melt the basil butter in a skillet and add the shrimp. Sauté for a minute or two, until the shrimp are pink and cooked through.

3. Put the warm pasta in a large bowl and pour the sauce over. Garnish with the extra Pecorino Romano cheese.

Serves 4

AT-HOME COST: $9.50

Substitute crab or chicken for the shrimp in this recipe.

OLIVE GARDEN
tuscan garlic chicken

HERB-CRUSTED CHICKEN BREASTS SAUTÉED UNTIL CRISP, SERVED OVER
FETTUCCINE PASTA, AND COVERED WITH A SPINACH-CREAM SAUCE.

1½ cups plus 1 tablespoon
all-purpose flour
1 tablespoon salt
2 teaspoons pepper
1 teaspoon dried marjoram
1 teaspoon chopped fresh basil
1 teaspoon dried oregano
6 boneless, skinless chicken breasts
or thighs
5 tablespoons extra virgin olive oil

1 tablespoon chopped garlic
1 red bell pepper, julienned
½ cup dry white wine
8 ounces spinach, stemmed
1½ cups heavy cream
1 cup grated Parmesan cheese
1 pound fettuccine, cooked
according to the package
directions

1. Preheat the oven to 350°F.

2. Combine the 1½ cups flour, the salt, pepper, marjoram, basil, and
   oregano. Dip each chicken breast in the flour mixture until well coated.

3. Heat 3 tablespoons of the olive oil in a skillet over medium heat and
   sauté the chicken for 2 to 3 minutes until golden on each side, turning
   once. Drain on paper towels and then place the breasts on a baking sheet
   and finish cooking in the oven for about 15 minutes, or until cooked
   through.

4. Heat the remaining 2 tablespoons olive oil in a saucepan and sauté the
   garlic and bell pepper. When the garlic is soft, start whisking in the
   1 tablespoon flour, stirring constantly until the flour is smooth and
   slightly browned.

5. Add the wine to the saucepan and bring to a low boil. Add the
   spinach and cream and stir until the spinach is just wilted. Stir in
   all but 1 tablespoon of the Parmesan cheese.

6. Toss the pasta with half of the cheese sauce and transfer to a warmed
   serving bowl. Put some pasta on each plate and top with a chicken

breast, then pour some of the remaining sauce over the top. Sprinkle the remaining 1 tablespoon Parmesan over the 6 servings.

Serves 6

AT-HOME COST: $6.50

Use whole wheat pasta in place of regular semolina pasta.

OUTBACK STEAKHOUSE

bloomin' onion

AN OUTBACK ORIGINAL! THEIR ONIONS ARE HAND-CARVED BY A DEDICATED BLOOMOLOGIST. EACH BLOOM IS COOKED UNTIL GOLDEN AND SERVED WITH THEIR SPICY DIPPING SAUCE.

Onion
4 Vidalia or Texas sweet onions

Batter
1/3 cup cornstarch
1 1/2 cups all-purpose flour
2 teaspoons minced garlic
2 teaspoons paprika
1 teaspoon salt
1 teaspoon black pepper
3 cups beer

Seasoned Flour
2 cups all-purpose flour
4 teaspoons paprika

2 teaspoons garlic powder
1/2 teaspoon black pepper
1/4 teaspoon cayenne pepper

Creamy Chili Sauce
2 cups mayonnaise
2 cups sour cream
1/2 cup chili sauce
1/2 teaspoon cayenne pepper

Special Equipment
Electric deep-fryer or a fry basket

Vegetable oil, for deep-frying,
    as needed

1. Do ahead: Cut ¾ inch off the tops of the onions and peel, cutting each onion into 12 to 16 vertical wedges without cutting all the way through the bottom root end. Remove about 1 inch of petals from the center of each onion. Refrigerate until ready to use.

2. Do ahead: Make the batter by whisking together the cornstarch, flour, garlic, paprika, salt, and black pepper. Gradually add the beer and whisk well. Set aside until ready to use.

3. Do ahead: Make the seasoned flour by combining all the dry ingredients. Set aside until ready to use.

4. Do ahead: Make the sauce by combining all the ingredients. Refrigerate until needed.

5. Heat the electric fryer to 375°F, or heat the oil in a sturdy pot with a fry basket that fits it, also to 375°F.

6. To fry, coat the onions with the seasoned flour and shake off the excess. Dip the onions in the beer batter, coating thoroughly. Carefully lower each onion, root side down, into the hot oil and fry until golden brown all over, turning once. Remove and drain on paper towels.

7. To serve, place the onions upright in shallow bowls. Remove the center cores with an apple corer. Serve while still hot with the creamy chili sauce on the side.

Serves 4

AT-HOME COST: $9

Outback Steakhouse was founded in Florida in 1987. At the time, the 1986 movie *Crocodile Dundee* had recently been released and had become a big hit. Despite the fact that none of the restaurant's founders had ever been to Australia, the trio decided to give their venture an Australian theme. The outback is the Wild West of Australia, and the restaurants strive to achieve that Aussie ambience.

OUTBACK STEAKHOUSE
mac a roo 'n' cheese

A HEARTY MAC-AND-CHEESE DISH WITH AN OLD-FASHIONED FLAVOR.

3 tablespoons butter
2 tablespoons all-purpose flour
1½ cups milk
¼ teaspoon salt
⅛ teaspoon paprika

8 ounces Velveeta cheese, cubed
12 ounces medium rigatoni pasta,
cooked according to the package
directions

1. Melt the butter in a medium saucepan and whisk in the flour, stirring to thicken. Do not let the butter brown. Whisk in the milk, salt, and paprika, then the cubes of Velveeta, incorporating them all until the sauce thickens. If it seems too thick, add a little more milk.

2. Add the cooked pasta to the sauce and serve warm.

Serves 2 or 3

AT-HOME COST: $4.50

PANDA EXPRESS

chow mein

CHOW MEIN PREPARED WITH WHOLE GRAIN NOODLES THAT ARE TOSSED IN THE
WOK WITH SHREDDED GREEN ONIONS, CELERY, CABBAGE, AND BEAN SPROUTS.

1 tablespoon vegetable oil
2 green onions, trimmed and cut
  crosswise into ½-inch-thick
  pieces
¼ cup sliced celery
1½ cups sliced Napa cabbage
¼ cup bean sprouts
¼ teaspoon sugar
½ cup chicken broth

1½ teaspoons soy sauce
1 teaspoon Asian sesame oil
1½ teaspoons cornstarch,
  dissolved in 1 tablespoon cold
  water
4 ounces thin whole grain noodles,
  cooked according to the package
  directions
Red pepper flakes

1. Heat the oil in a wok or large skillet and stir-fry the green onions, celery,
   cabbage, and bean sprouts for about 3 minutes, or until the cabbage is
   wilted. Add the sugar, broth, soy sauce, and sesame oil and simmer,
   covered, for 3 minutes.

2. Stir in the mixture of cornstarch and water and bring the contents of the
   wok to a boil—the sauce will thicken.

3. Serve over the whole grain noodles and season with red pepper flakes.

Serves 1

AT-HOME COST: $6

Panda Express is the fastest-growing Chinese fast-food chain in
North America, serving authentic Chinese stir-fried dishes.

PANDA EXPRESS
garlic chicken breasts with string beans

CHICKEN BREASTS MARINATED WITH AN ASIAN TOUCH, STIR-FRIED WITH GREEN BEANS, AND SERVED OVER YOUR CHOICE OF RICE OR NOODLES.

2 tablespoons soy sauce
2 teaspoons rice wine vinegar
1 teaspoon Asian sesame oil
2 teaspoons cornstarch
1 teaspoon sugar
1 pound boneless, skinless chicken breasts, cut into 1/4-inch strips
2 tablespoons vegetable oil
1 large onion, peeled and cut into 1/2-inch wedges

2 tablespoons minced garlic
1 teaspoon black bean sauce
12 ounces green beans, cut into 3-inch pieces
1 cup coarsely diced red bell pepper
Hot cooked rice or noodles, for serving

1. Do ahead: Combine the soy sauce with the rice wine vinegar, sesame oil, cornstarch, and sugar. Whisk to blend all the ingredients. Add the chicken strips and toss to coat well. Refrigerate, covered, for about 20 minutes.

2. Heat the vegetable oil in a wok or large skillet and stir-fry the chicken for about 3 minutes, or until the chicken begins to brown and is cooked through. Remove the cooked chicken from the wok and keep warm.

3. To the same wok, add the onion, garlic, and black bean sauce. Quickly add the green beans and bell pepper. Add 1/4 cup water, cover, and cook for 3 minutes, or until the vegetables are crisp-tender. Return the chicken to the wok and stir-fry quickly to combine the flavors. Serve over rice or noodles.

Serves 4

AT-HOME COST: $9.50

PANDA EXPRESS

spicy chicken

CHICKEN, ONION, BELL PEPPER, SQUASH, AND PEANUTS TOSSED WITH A SLIGHTLY SWEET AND SPICY SAUCE. THIS DISH IS SPICY HOT! IF YOU PREFER A LESS SPICY DISH, DECREASE THE AMOUNTS OF DRIED CHILE AND RED PEPPER FLAKES.

½ cup diced chayote squash
½ cup vegetable oil
12 ounces chicken, diced
Salt and black pepper
⅓ cup diced onion
¼ cup diced red bell pepper
8 pieces whole dried chile pepper
½ teaspoon minced fresh ginger
½ teaspoon minced garlic

1½ teaspoons red pepper flakes, or to taste
½ teaspoon Shao Hsing wine
1 teaspoon soy sauce
2 tablespoons chicken broth
1 teaspoon sugar
Dash of Asian sesame oil
1 tablespoon cornstarch
¼ cup roasted peanuts

1. Do ahead: Blanch the diced chayote for a minute in a steamer or boiling water, then drain and set aside.

2. Heat ¼ cup of the vegetable oil in a wok or skillet and add the chicken, seasoned with salt and black pepper. Stir-fry until cooked through, then add the onion and bell pepper and cook until the vegetables are crisp-tender. Drain the vegetables with the chicken and set aside.

3. In the same wok, heat the remaining ¼ cup oil and stir-fry the chile pepper, ginger, and garlic until slightly soft. Add the red pepper flakes, Shao Hsing wine, soy sauce, chicken broth, sugar, and sesame oil. Bring to a boil and whisk in the cornstarch.

4. Add the cooked chicken mixture and blanched chayote and toss with the other ingredients to combine. Toss in the peanuts and serve warm.

Serves 1

AT-HOME COST: $6.50

Chayote is a squash frequently found in markets featuring Latin and Asian produce. Its soft pit should be scooped out before or after cooking. It can be eaten with the skin on and has a sweet, buttery flavor. You may substitute zucchini.

Substitute medium-dry sherry if you can't find Shao Hsing wine.

PANERA BREAD

apple-sausage patties with sage

SAGE-FLAVORED PORK SAUSAGE PATTIES STUDDED WITH FRESH APPLE BITS, SERVED OVER SOURDOUGH BREAD SLICES.

2 tablespoons finely chopped onion
1 Granny Smith apple, peeled and finely diced
1 teaspoon olive oil
3 cloves garlic, minced
½ teaspoon ground ginger
1 teaspoon minced fresh thyme, or ½ teaspoon dried
1 tablespoon minced fresh sage, or 1 teaspoon dried
¼ teaspoon salt
¼ teaspoon pepper
1 pound pork, coarsely ground
1 egg white, beaten
1 small loaf Panera sourdough bread, or similar bread of your choice, sliced into 12 pieces
Dijon mustard, for serving

1. Do ahead: Sauté the onion and apple in the olive oil until just softened, then add the garlic and ground ginger, herbs, salt, and pepper. Set aside to cool before using.

2. Combine the apple mixture with the ground pork and the egg white. Blend the mixture well, making sure the egg white is evenly distributed. Shape into 12 patties.

3. Heat a nonstick skillet and sauté the patties until they are cooked through, turning once.

4. Serve on the sliced sourdough bread with Dijon mustard on the side.

Serves 12 as an appetizer or 6 as an entrée

AT-HOME COST: $9.50

Panera started as Au Bon Pain Company. Established in 1981 with the single goal of making great bread broadly available to consumers across America, Panera Bread understands that great bread makes great meals, from made-to-order sandwiches to tossed-to-order salads to soup served in bread bowls.

PANERA BREAD

baked bread-and-cabbage soup with smoked sausage

A CASSEROLE OF CABBAGE WITH LAYERS OF HEARTY BREAD, CHEESE, AND SAUSAGE.

1 head green cabbage, halved
1 bay leaf
5 tablespoons butter, softened
3 slices country-style bread, preferably day-old Panera, or similar bread of your choice (see Note)
3 slices whole wheat bread, preferably day-old Panera, or similar bread of your choice

Salt and pepper
1½ cups coarsely grated Fontina cheese
½ cup coarsely grated Swiss cheese
3 cups beef broth
8 ounces smoked beef sausage, sliced into ½-inch rounds

1. Remove the core and tough stem pieces from the halved cabbage and slice into thick strips. Blanch the cabbage with the bay leaf in boiling water just until tender. Discard the bay leaf and drain the cabbage. Set aside until ready to use.

2. Spread 4 tablespoons of the butter on both sides of the bread slices. Heat a large skillet and toast the bread on both sides until golden brown.

3. Preheat the oven to 350°F.

4. Line the bottom of a 10-cup soufflé dish with the bread. Place half the cabbage over the bread and season with salt and pepper. Sprinkle with ¾ cup of the Fontina cheese and all of the Swiss cheese. Repeat the layering with the whole wheat bread, the remaining cabbage, salt and pepper, and the remaining ¾ cup Fontina cheese. Dot with the remaining 1 tablespoon butter.

5. Carefully pour the broth over the bread and cabbage and bake the casserole for about 45 minutes, or until the top is golden brown.

6. Heat the sausage slices in a skillet until cooked through. To serve, ladle the soup into warmed bowls and float a couple of the sausage slices on top.

Note: If you are using a bread other than Panera, make sure the slices are ½ inch thick and measure about 3 by 5 inches.

Serves 4 to 6

AT-HOME COST: $8.50

PANERA BREAD
chicken breasts with herbed crust

LIGHTLY SEASONED, CITRUS-INFUSED CHICKEN BREASTS BREADED IN SOUR-
DOUGH CRUMBS AND FRESH HERBS.

8 boneless, skinless chicken
breasts

½ cup lemon juice

2 cups dry bread crumbs made
from Panera sourdough bread or
a similar bread of your choice

⅓ cup chopped fresh basil

¼ cup chopped fresh parsley

2 tablespoons chopped fresh
rosemary

1½ teaspoons salt

½ teaspoon pepper

3 tablespoons butter

2 tablespoons olive oil

Lemon wedges, for garnish

1. Do ahead: Pound the chicken breasts between 2 sheets of plastic wrap to
   a thickness of about ½ inch. Place the breasts in a shallow bowl, pour
   the lemon juice over the pounded chicken, and refrigerate, covered, for
   1 hour.

2. Do ahead: Combine the bread crumbs, basil, parsley, rosemary, salt, and
   pepper, and set aside.

3. Preheat the oven to 450°F. Place foil on a baking sheet and set aside.

4. Melt the butter with the oil in a small pan or the microwave.

5. Take the breasts out of the lemon juice and pat dry. Brush each breast
   with the butter-oil mixture, then coat both sides with the seasoned bread
   crumbs. Lay the breasts on the prepared baking sheet and bake for about
   20 minutes, or until the crust is golden and the chicken is cooked
   through—no pink meat, and the juices run clear.

6. Serve on a warmed platter with lemon wedges as garnish.

Serves 8

AT-HOME COST: $9.50

Substitute boneless pork chops for the chicken in this recipe.

PANERA BREAD
crispy zucchini rounds

SEASONED ZUCCHINI SLICES, WITH A LIGHT TOPPING OF PARMESAN CHEESE AND BREAD CRUMBS.

3 to 4 medium zucchini
1/3 cup dry bread crumbs made from Panera ciabatta or a similar bread of your choice
1/3 cup grated Parmesan cheese

1/2 teaspoon garlic powder
Pinch of ground ginger
Salt and pepper
1/4 cup olive oil

1. Preheat the broiler.

2. Cut the zucchini into 1/2-inch slices, on the diagonal. Combine the bread crumbs and Parmesan cheese.

3. Season the zucchini with the garlic powder, ginger, and salt and pepper. Sauté the zucchini lightly in the olive oil. The slices should be light brown, but still crisp-tender.

4. Transfer to a baking dish and top with the crumb-and-cheese mixture. Broil just until the topping is slightly browned and crusty. Serve warm.

Serves 4 to 6

AT-HOME COST: $5

PANERA BREAD
french bread pizza

AN EASY-TO-MAKE PIZZA FOR SNACKING, FOR LUNCH, OR EVEN FOR DINNER—
JUST ADD A SIDE SALAD.

I loaf Panera French bread, or similar bread of your choice
Butter
1½ cups tomato sauce, homemade or store-bought

½ cup shredded fresh basil leaves
2 large Roma tomatoes, sliced
Salt and pepper
8 ounces mozzarella cheese, sliced

1. Preheat the oven to 475°F.
2. Cut the bread in half lengthwise and butter the cut sides.
3. Bake the halves on a baking sheet until lightly toasted, about 5 minutes.
4. Spread the tomato sauce over the toasted halves, sprinkle with the basil, and top with the tomato slices; season with salt and pepper. Layer the cheese slices over the tomatoes. Bake for 12 to 15 minutes, until the cheese begins to brown and bubble.
5. Cut into pieces and serve hot.

Serves 6

AT-HOME COST: $9

PANERA BREAD

grilled italian salad with prosciutto chips

A GRILLED VEGETABLE-AND-BREAD SALAD TOPPED WITH CRUNCHY BAKED PROSCIUTTO.

2 or 3 slices prosciutto
4 slices Panera sourdough bread, or similar bread of your choice
One 14-ounce can cannellini beans
1 medium red bell pepper, seeded and quartered
1 medium tomato, cut into ½-inch-thick slices
2 thickly cut onion slices (about 1½ inches)
¼ cup olive oil vinaigrette, home-made or store-bought
¼ cup shredded fresh basil leaves
1½ teaspoons lemon juice
Salt and pepper

1. Preheat the oven to 350°F.

2. Do ahead: Lay the prosciutto slices in a single layer on a baking sheet and bake, undisturbed, for 25 to 30 minutes. They should be crispy and dry. Leave them on the baking sheet and set aside.

3. Do ahead: Cut the sourdough bread into 3 by 5-inch rectangles, ½ inch thick. Drain and rinse the cannellini beans. Set aside.

4. Preheat the grill or broiler.

5. Put the vegetables and bread pieces on a baking sheet and brush every-thing, on both sides, with half the vinaigrette. Grill the bread until toasted on both sides; then grill the vegetables until slightly browned and crisp-tender, turning once.

6. Dice all the grilled vegetables and the bread into bite-size pieces and put in a salad bowl. Add the cannellini beans, basil, and the remaining vinaigrette with the lemon juice. Season with salt and pepper and toss

lightly. Gently crumble the slices of prosciutto and serve the salad on individual plates. Garnish with the prosciutto.

Serves 2

AT-HOME COST: $9.50

PANERA BREAD
strawberry and brie bruschetta

SOURDOUGH SLICES TOASTED AND SPREAD WITH A BLEND OF SWEETENED STRAWBERRIES AND BRIE, TOPPED WITH ALMONDS.

⅓ cup packed light brown sugar
2 teaspoons ground cinnamon
4 to 5 cups sliced strawberries
½ teaspoon vanilla extract
½ cup sliced almonds
5⅓ tablespoons butter, softened

1 Panera sourdough baguette, or similar bread of your choice, sliced into 12 pieces
One 12-ounce wheel Brie cheese, cut into 12 slices

1. Do ahead: Combine the brown sugar and cinnamon. Toss the sliced strawberries and vanilla extract with half the cinnamon mixture. Set aside.

2. Preheat the oven to 375°F.

3. Lay the almonds on a sheet pan and bake until lightly toasted, about 5 minutes, shaking the pan frequently. Let cool and set aside.

4. Butter 1 side of each piece of bread. Sprinkle with the remaining half of the cinnamon mixture on the buttered side. Lay the bread pieces on a baking sheet and toast for about 5 minutes.

5. Put 1 slice of Brie on each piece of bread and return the bread to the oven for another 4 to 5 minutes, until the Brie is slightly melted.

6. Put the bread slices on a serving platter and spoon some of the strawberry mixture over each piece. Top with the sliced almonds.

Serves 4 to 6

AT-HOME COST: $8

Substitute fat-free cream cheese for the Brie.

PANERA BREAD
vegetarian creamy tomato soup

SEASONED TOMATOES PUREED TO A VELVETY SMOOTH TEXTURE, ENHANCED WITH ONION AND OREGANO.

5 tablespoons butter
1/2 cup chopped onion
5 tablespoons all-purpose flour
4 cups half-and-half
1/2 bay leaf
1 1/2 teaspoons salt

1/2 teaspoon pepper
1 1/2 teaspoons sugar
1/2 teaspoon dried oregano
1/2 teaspoon baking soda
One 15-ounce can peeled whole tomatoes, crushed, with juice

1. In a stockpot, heat the butter and sauté the onion, stirring until it is softened, but not browned. Whisk in the flour and stir constantly until the paste is smooth, 1 to 2 minutes. Do not let the flour get brown.

2. Gradually add the half-and-half, then the bay leaf, salt, pepper, sugar, and oregano. Simmer until the soup is slightly thickened.

3. Stir the baking soda into the tomatoes, then add the tomatoes to the soup. Simmer for a few minutes to let the flavors blend. Remove the bay leaf, puree the soup in a blender or with an immersion blender, reheat briefly, and serve in warmed bowls.

Serves 6

AT-HOME COST: $5.00

PANERA BREAD

zucchini parmesan

A ZUCCHINI-AND-ONION MEDLEY WITH A BREAD CRUMB AND PARMESAN TOPPING, SMOTHERED IN TOMATO SAUCE.

3 or 4 large zucchini
¼ cup olive oil
1 large onion, thinly sliced
⅓ cup shredded fresh basil leaves
½ teaspoon garlic powder
Salt and pepper

½ cup grated Parmesan cheese
½ cup dry bread crumbs from Panera French bread or ciabatta, or a similar bread of your choice
One 15-ounce can tomato sauce

1. Cut the zucchini into ½-inch-thick rounds. Sauté in a large skillet with the olive oil until slightly browned on both sides but still crisp-tender.

2. Preheat the oven to 350°F.

3. Layer the zucchini in a 9 by 13-inch baking dish with the onion slices, basil, garlic powder, salt and pepper, and Parmesan cheese; finish with the bread crumbs. Pour the tomato sauce over the whole casserole and bake for 45 minutes, or until all the vegetables are cooked through.

Serves 6

AT-HOME COST: $6.50

PEPPERIDGE FARM
milano cookies

RICH DARK CHOCOLATE SANDWICHED BETWEEN TWO LAYERS OF SHORTBREAD.

Chocolate Sauce
1 cup semisweet chocolate
chips
1 tablespoon salted butter

Shortbread Cookies
¾ cup packed light brown sugar
½ pound (2 sticks) salted butter,
softened
2 teaspoons vanilla extract
2 cups all-purpose flour

1. Preheat the oven to 325°F. Line baking sheets with parchment paper and set aside.

2. To make the chocolate sauce, melt the chocolate chips and the 1 tablespoon butter in the top of a double boiler, being careful not to let it get too hot—if overheated, the chocolate will burn and the butter will separate. Set aside at room temperature until ready to use.

3. Cream the sugar and the butter until light and fluffy. Add the vanilla extract and the flour, 1 cup at a time, and stir until well incorporated.

4. Shape the dough into twenty 1-inch balls and press them into 2-inch-long ovals. Place the cookies 2 inches apart on the baking sheets and bake for 17 to 20 minutes, until golden. Remove from the oven and let the cookies cool completely.

5. Dip the flat side of each cookie into the chocolate sauce and press the 2 chocolate sides together to make a "sandwich." Let the cookies rest on a cooled baking sheet until the chocolate hardens a little.

Makes 10 cookies

AT-HOME COST: $4.50

Add ground pecans or walnuts to the chocolate before dipping.

Margaret Rudkin founded Pepperidge Farm (named after her family farm in Fairfield, Connecticut) in 1937, selling homemade bread and rolls. The brand has since added cookies, crackers, stuffing mixes, Texas toast, and frozen pastries, as well as many other frozen items.

P.F. CHANG'S CHINA BISTRO
coconut-curry vegetables

STIR-FRIED MIXED VEGETABLES AND CRISPY TOFU IN A COCONUT-CURRY SAUCE.

Coconut-Curry Sauce
½ cup coconut milk
2 tablespoons soy sauce
½ teaspoon curry powder
1½ to 2 tablespoons packed dark brown sugar
2 teaspoons rice wine vinegar

1 pound firm tofu
3 cups broccoli florets

1 cup thinly sliced carrots
2 teaspoons Asian sesame oil
1 small onion, cut into ¾-inch dice
1 small red bell pepper, seeded and cut into ¾-inch dice
1 cup mushrooms, cut in half
2 teaspoons cornstarch

1. Do ahead: To make the coconut-curry sauce, combine all the sauce ingredients in a small saucepan and mix well. Set aside.

2. Do ahead: Drain the tofu and wrap it in a clean dish towel. Put a plate on top of the wrapped tofu to compress it and release the excess water. Let it rest for about 30 minutes, then unwrap it and slice it into 4 equal pieces; set aside.

3. Do ahead: Slightly blanch the broccoli florets and sliced carrots, then shock in ice water to stop the cooking. Drain and set aside.

4. Heat the sesame oil in a wok or skillet and stir-fry the tofu for about 2 minutes. Add the onion and bell pepper, and stir-fry until crisp-tender, 3 to 4 minutes. Add the mushrooms and stir-fry for 2 minutes, then add the blanched broccoli and carrots. Keep warm in the wok.

5. Bring the coconut-curry sauce to a simmer, stirring to blend well. Mix 1½ tablespoons of water with the cornstarch. Whisk briskly into the coconut-curry sauce and stir until the sauce thickens, about 15 seconds. Pour the sauce over the tofu and vegetables, tossing well. Serve warm.

Serves 2 to 4

AT-HOME COST: $8.50

You might want to substitute 1 cup sugar snap peas for the carrots. Blanch them just slightly. Coconut milk is available at larger markets and wherever Asian and Latin foods are sold.

P.F. Chang's China Bistro is unique. It blends classic Chinese design with a modern bistro look. Each location features an original hand-painted mural depicting scenes of life in twelfth-century China. Each P.F. Chang's meal is meant to attain harmony of taste, texture, color, and aroma by balancing the Chinese principles of *fan* and *t'sai*. *Fan* foods include rice, noodles, grains, and dumplings, while vegetables, meat, poultry, and seafood are *t'sai* foods.

P.F. CHANG'S CHINA BISTRO
garlic noodles

EGG NOODLES TOSSED WITH GARLIC AND CHILE PEPPER, STIR-FRIED WITH CANTONESE SAUCE.

Garnish
1 English cucumber

Cantonese Stir-Fry Sauce
¾ cup water
1 tablespoon chicken bouillon powder
1 tablespoon sugar
1 tablespoon Shao Hsing wine
1 tablespoon oyster sauce
½ teaspoon salt
1 teaspoon cornstarch

Garlic Noodles
1 tablespoon minced garlic
2 tablespoons chopped chile pepper
2 tablespoons canola oil
1 tablespoon sugar
2 tablespoons white vinegar
1 pound fresh Chinese noodles or vermicelli, cooked according to the package directions
½ teaspoon red pepper flakes
2 tablespoons chopped fresh cilantro
½ teaspoon Asian sesame oil

1. Do ahead: Slice the cucumber into ¼-inch-thick slices, then cut each slice into strips. Set aside.

2. Do ahead: Make the Cantonese sauce by combining all the sauce ingredients in a small bowl and whisking to blend well. Set aside.

3. Heat a wok or skillet and stir-fry the garlic and chile pepper in the canola oil, about 1 minute. Do not let the garlic burn. Add the sugar and vinegar and stir to blend. Add the cooked noodles with the red pepper flakes and cilantro, then add ½ cup of the Cantonese sauce. Drizzle the sesame oil over everything in the wok and stir to mix, allowing the sauce to thicken. Serve on individual plates and garnish with the strips of cucumber.

AT-HOME COST: $7.50

Substitute medium-dry sherry if you can't find Shao Hsing wine.

P.F. CHANG'S CHINA BISTRO
ginger chicken with broccoli

CHICKEN SERVED CANTONESE-STYLE ON A BED OF STEAMED FRESH BROCCOLI.

Chicken

2 large eggs, beaten
2 tablespoons cornstarch
2 tablespoons vegetable oil
¼ teaspoon white pepper
¼ teaspoon salt
1 pound boneless, skinless chicken breasts, sliced

Stir-Fry Sauce

½ cup tamari or soy sauce
2 tablespoons rice wine vinegar
2 tablespoons sugar
½ cup chicken broth

3 cups chicken broth or water
8 ounces broccoli florets
3 tablespoons vegetable oil
2 tablespoons minced peeled fresh ginger
2 tablespoons minced green onion
1 teaspoon minced garlic
¼ cup cornstarch
1 teaspoon Asian sesame oil
Steamed rice or noodles, for serving

1. Do ahead: Marinate the chicken. Combine the eggs, cornstarch, vegetable oil, white pepper, and salt. Add the chicken pieces and marinate, covered, in the refrigerator for at least 3 hours. Drain well when ready to use. Discard the marinade.

2. Do ahead: Combine the ingredients for the stir-fry sauce and set aside.

3. Bring the 3 cups chicken broth to a boil in a wok or skillet, then reduce to a simmer. Add the drained pieces of marinated chicken and cook not quite all the way through. Remove the chicken from the pot, drain, and keep warm.

4. Put the broccoli in the simmering chicken broth and cook until crisp-tender. Drain and arrange in a ring on a serving platter and keep warm. Discard the broth and wipe the wok clean.

5. Heat the wok again and add the 3 tablespoons vegetable oil. Add the ginger, green onion, and garlic, sautéing for just a few seconds. Add the stir-fry sauce and simmer for a few minutes.

6. Add the reserved chicken and cook all the way through, 2 to 4 minutes. Mix the ¼ cup cornstarch with ½ cup water and add to the simmering wok. Stir in the sesame oil. When the sauce has thickened, pour the stir-fry into the center of the broccoli ring. Serve with steamed rice or noodles.

Serves 3 or 4

AT-HOME COST: $7

Tamari is a soy sauce with little or no added wheat.

P.F. CHANG'S CHINA BISTRO
lemon-pepper shrimp

SHRIMP TOSSED IN A TANGY SAUCE AND SERVED ON A BED OF LEEKS AND BEAN SPROUTS.

Black Pepper Sauce
3 tablespoons black pepper
3 tablespoons minced garlic
½ cup tomato ketchup
¼ cup soy sauce
1½ cups chicken broth
¼ cup plus 2 tablespoons sugar

1 cup canola oil
12 medium shrimp, peeled and
   deveined
2 tablespoons cornstarch
2 leeks, white parts only, julienned
8 ounces bean sprouts
1 lemon half, cut into thin slices

1. Do ahead: Combine the black pepper sauce ingredients and set aside until ready to use, or store in a covered container in the refrigerator.

2. In a wok or heavy saucepan, heat the canola oil to 365°F. Lightly dust the shrimp in the cornstarch and fry until the cornstarch is puffy and slightly golden and the shrimp are pink throughout. Drain on paper towels. Discard all but 1 tablespoon of the oil.

3. Heat the tablespoon of reserved oil in the wok and stir-fry the leeks and bean sprouts for about 1 minute—do not overcook. Remove the vegetables from the wok. Add the lemon slices to the wok and heat through, then add the shrimp back to the wok and add as much black pepper sauce as desired—you do not have to use the whole amount.

4. Arrange the leeks and the bean sprouts on a serving platter and pour the shrimp and lemon-pepper sauce mixture on top.

Serves 4

AT-HOME COST: $8.50

P.F. CHANG'S CHINA BISTRO
mongolian beef

STIR-FRIED FLANK STEAK WITH GINGER AND GARLIC—P.F. CHANG'S SIGNATURE DISH.

Sauce

2 teaspoons vegetable oil

½ teaspoon minced peeled fresh ginger

1 tablespoon chopped garlic

¾ cup packed dark brown sugar

½ cup soy sauce

1 pound flank steak

¼ cup cornstarch

1 cup vegetable oil

2 large green onions, sliced

1. Do ahead: To make the sauce, heat the 2 teaspoons vegetable oil in a medium saucepan and sauté the ginger and garlic, stirring constantly. Do not let the garlic burn. Add the brown sugar, soy sauce, and ½ cup of water. Dissolve the brown sugar by whisking vigorously. Bring the mixture to a boil and let the sauce thicken, then set it aside until ready to use, or let it cool before covering and refrigerating.

2. Slice the flank steak into ¼-inch-thick pieces. Be sure to cut against the grain of the meat so that it remains tender. Coat each piece lightly in the cornstarch and refrigerate for about 10 minutes.

3. Heat the 1 cup vegetable oil in a wok or large skillet. Add the beef, working in batches, and fry until each piece is slightly golden brown. Remove to paper towels and let drain. Discard the oil.

4. Heat the wok over medium heat and return the meat to stir-fry for 1 minute. Add the sauce and simmer for 1 minute, then add the green onions. Stir-fry for another minute, then transfer to a serving platter.

Serves 4

AT-HOME COST: $6.50

P.F. CHANG'S CHINA BISTRO
oolong-marinated sea bass

A GREAT CATCH STEEPED IN OOLONG TEA, THEN BROILED—SERVED WITH A SWEET GINGER SAUCE AND SPINACH.

⅔ cup soy sauce
¾ cup packed light brown sugar
2 teaspoons minced peeled fresh ginger
½ teaspoon loose oolong tea leaves
1½ teaspoons minced garlic

Two 8-ounce sea bass fillets
1 tablespoon vegetable oil
6 cups fresh spinach
6 to 8 ears canned baby corn, drained
Salt and pepper

1. Do ahead: Marinate the sea bass. Combine 2 cups water, the soy sauce, brown sugar, ginger, tea leaves, and 1 teaspoon of the garlic in a small saucepan and bring to a boil, then reduce the heat and simmer for 5 minutes. Strain through a fine-mesh strainer to remove the ginger, tea leaves, and garlic. Let the sauce cool completely before adding the fish fillets. Put 2 cups of the marinade in a resealable plastic bag and add the fillets. Marinate, refrigerated, for 5 to 7 hours, turning occasionally to cover the fish.

2. Preheat the oven to 425°F.

3. Remove the fillets from the marinade and place them in a baking dish. Discard the marinade in the bag. Bake the fillets for about 20 minutes, or until the edges start to turn brown.

4. Turn off the oven and preheat the broiler.

5. While waiting for the broiler, heat the oil in a wok or large skillet and quickly stir-fry the spinach, the remaining ½ teaspoon garlic, and the baby corn just until the spinach is wilted and the baby corn is warm. Season with salt and pepper and divide between 2 plates; keep warm.

6. Put the sea bass under the broiler for just a couple of minutes, or until the sugar in the marinade begins to caramelize. The fish is through cooking, so you are just browning the top.

Serves 2

AT-HOME COST: $9.50

Experiment with different teas to make this dish your own!

P.F. CHANG'S CHINA BISTRO
orange peel chicken

STIR-FRIED CHICKEN WITH JALAPEÑO CHILE PEPPER AND ORANGE PEEL MAKES
FOR A SPICY-CITRUS COMBINATION.

Sauce
1 tablespoon vegetable oil
2 tablespoons minced garlic
4 green onions, sliced
1 cup tomato sauce, homemade
   or store-bought
¼ cup sugar
2 tablespoons chili garlic paste
1 jalapeño pepper, chopped
1 tablespoon soy sauce

Chicken
1 egg, beaten
1 cup milk
1 cup all-purpose flour
4 boneless, skinless chicken
   breasts, cut into bite-size pieces
½ cup vegetable oil
Zest of ¼ orange, julienned

Cooked white or brown rice, for
   serving (optional)

1. Do ahead: To make the sauce, heat the 1 tablespoon vegetable oil in a small saucepan and sauté the garlic and green onions for 1 minute, then add the tomato sauce and bring to a boil. Add the sugar, chili garlic paste, jalapeño, and soy sauce. Simmer for about 5 minutes, or until the sauce has thickened. Remove from the heat and set aside, or let cool and refrigerate, covered, until ready to use.

2. Combine the egg and milk and whisk together until thoroughly mixed. Put the flour in a shallow bowl. Dip the chicken pieces first in the flour, then in the milk-and-egg mixture, then again in the flour. Place the coated chicken on a baking sheet in a single layer and refrigerate for about 10 minutes to set the coating.

3. Heat the ½ cup vegetable oil in a wok or large skillet and sauté the chicken, in batches, until slightly golden brown and cooked through (no longer pink in the middle). When done, drain the cooked chicken on paper towels and keep warm.

4. Discard the oil in the wok and wipe down the pan. Add the orange zest and heat through for 1 minute, then add the sauce and heat it through. Add the cooked chicken to the wok and heat through, stirring well to coat all the pieces with the sauce. Serve with cooked rice, if desired.

Serves 4

AT-HOME COST: $7

P.F. CHANG'S CHINA BISTRO
red sauce wontons

WONTONS FILLED WITH SHRIMP AND PORK, COVERED IN A SPICY ASIAN SAUCE.

Sauce
1 cup soy sauce
3 tablespoons white vinegar
1½ tablespoons chili oil
½ teaspoon chili garlic paste
3 tablespoons sugar
½ teaspoon minced fresh garlic
Asian sesame oil, to taste

Wonton Filling
8 ounces shrimp, peeled, deveined, and finely minced
4 ounces pork, trimmed and finely minced
2 tablespoons finely minced carrot

2 tablespoons finely minced green onion
1 teaspoon minced peeled fresh ginger
2 tablespoons oyster sauce
¼ teaspoon Asian sesame oil

8 wonton wrappers
All-purpose flour or cornstarch, for dusting
1 cup chicken broth

Garnish
Chopped green onions
Chopped fresh cilantro

1. Do ahead: To make the sauce, in a medium saucepan, combine all the sauce ingredients and simmer for 5 minutes, then set aside or let cool and refrigerate, covered, until ready to use.

2. The wonton filling needs to be very finely minced. If you cannot get everything small enough, put the shrimp, pork, carrot, green onion, and ginger in a food processor and pulse until the ingredients resemble a paste, then add the oyster sauce and sesame oil. If you're able to mince everything by hand, combine all the ingredients in a bowl and mix well with a wooden spoon until the mixture is like a paste.

3. Place a teaspoon of filling in the center of each wonton wrapper. Wet your finger and run it around the edges of the wrapper. Pull the corners

up until they meet, and pinch together the dampened seams. Refrigerate for 10 minutes on a dish dusted with flour or cornstarch. This will keep the moist wontons from sticking to the dish.

4. In a small saucepan, bring the chicken broth to a low boil. Add the wontons, two at a time, and let cook until they float to the top. The wrappers should be translucent and the filling cooked through. Remove with a slotted spoon and place 2 wontons in each of 4 bowls. Pour some of the warmed sauce over the wontons and garnish with green onions and cilantro. Reserve the remainder of the sauce for another use.

Serves 4

AT-HOME COST: $7.50

P.F. CHANG'S CHINA BISTRO
roasted chicken, cantonese style

HONEY-GLAZED ROASTED CHICKEN WITH A HINT OF GINGER. PLEASE NOTE THAT YOU NEED TO PLAN AHEAD IF YOU WANT TO PREPARE THIS DISH: SEE STEPS 3 AND 4.

3 tablespoons baking soda
One 4-pound whole chicken
½ cup diced peeled fresh ginger
2 tablespoons Chinese five-spice powder
3 green onions, whole
5 star anise

¼ cup plus 2 tablespoons prepared black bean sauce
Grated zest of 1 whole orange

Glaze
2 tablespoons honey
3 tablespoons white vinegar

1. Dissolve the baking soda in 4 cups water. Place the chicken in a large bowl and pour the mixture over and inside the chicken, then rinse and pat dry, inside and out.

2. Combine the diced ginger, five-spice powder, green onions, star anise, black bean sauce, and orange zest and stuff the cavity of the chicken. Tie the legs together with kitchen string. This will "truss" the opening and keep the stuffing inside.

3. Make room in your refrigerator so that the chicken can be stood upright on its neck cavity and air-dried for 3 days. Stand the chicken up by placing it, neck-side-down, in a high-sided bowl. Or, if you have wire shelving in your refrigerator, tie a loop of string around the trussed legs and suspend the chicken over a plate to catch drips.

4. To glaze the chicken, mix the honey and vinegar, and with a pastry brush, baste the chicken twice a day for 3 days with the sauce.

5. Preheat the oven to 350°F.

6. Roast the chicken for 1½ to 2 hours—the juices should run clear and the internal temperature should reach 170°F. Carve and serve.

Serves 4

AT-HOME COST: $6.50

Black bean sauce is a highly concentrated paste of beans, garlic, soy, and other ingredients. It's used as a flavor enhancer and is often added to sweet and buttery ingredients for balance.

P.F. CHANG'S CHINA BISTRO
shrimp dumplings

MADE FRESH BY HAND, HERE SERVED STEAMED. YOU CAN ALSO PANFRY THEM.

Dipping Sauce
1 cup soy sauce
3 tablespoons white
  vinegar
½ teaspoon chili garlic
  paste
1 tablespoon sugar
½ teaspoon minced peeled
  fresh ginger
1 cup water
1 teaspoon chopped fresh
  cilantro

Wonton Filling
1 pound medium shrimp, peeled
  and deveined

2 tablespoons finely minced
  carrot
2 tablespoons finely minced
  green onion
1 teaspoon minced peeled
  fresh ginger
2 tablespoons oyster sauce
¼ teaspoon Asian sesame oil

One 1-pound package wonton
  wrappers
All-purpose flour or cornstarch,
  for dusting

1. Do ahead: To make the dipping sauce, combine all the sauce ingredients and mix well. Set aside until ready to use.

2. Separate the shrimp and grind half of them in a food processor. Chop the remaining shrimp into tiny dice. Mix together in a bowl with the remaining filling ingredients.

3. Put a heaped teaspoon of filling in the center of each wonton wrapper. Wet your finger in water and run it around the edges of the wrapper. Pull the corners up until they meet, and pinch the dampened seams together. Place on a plate dusted with a little flour or cornstarch and cover until ready to cook.

4. Steam the dumplings in a metal or bamboo steamer for 7 to 10 minutes. The wrappers should be translucent and the filling should be cooked through. Serve with the dipping sauce on the side.

Serves 2

AT-HOME COST: $5

P.F. CHANG'S CHINA BISTRO
spicy chicken

LIGHTLY STIR-FRIED IN A SWEET SZECHUAN SAUCE. THIS IS ANOTHER VERSION OF GENERAL TSO'S CHICKEN, AND ALWAYS A FAVORITE.

Sauce
2 teaspoons vegetable oil
2 tablespoons chopped garlic
3 tablespoons chopped green onion
1 cup pineapple juice
2 tablespoons chili garlic paste
2 tablespoons white vinegar
4 teaspoons sugar

1 teaspoon soy sauce
1/2 teaspoon cornstarch

1 cup vegetable oil
2 boneless, skinless chicken breasts, cut into bite-size pieces
1/3 cup cornstarch
Steamed or fried rice, for serving (optional)

1. Do ahead: To make the sauce, heat the 2 teaspoons vegetable oil in a small saucepan and sauté the garlic and green onion just until the garlic is soft. Add the pineapple juice, chili garlic paste, white vinegar, sugar, and soy sauce. Bring to a boil.

2. Mix 2 tablespoons water and the cornstarch together and add to the pan. Lower the heat to a simmer and let the sauce thicken. Set aside, or let cool and then refrigerate in a covered container until ready to use.

3. Heat the 1 cup vegetable oil in a wok or large skillet. Toss the chicken pieces with the 1/3 cup cornstarch and stir-fry until light brown. Drain on paper towels. Discard the oil in the wok. Add the sauce to the wok and heat through. Add the chicken pieces and toss with the sauce. Transfer to a large platter. Serve with steamed or fried rice, if desired.

Serves 2

AT-HOME COST: $5

P.F. CHANG'S CHINA BISTRO
stir-fried spicy eggplant

CUBES OF EGGPLANT TOSSED WITH GREEN ONIONS IN A SAVORY CHILE PEPPER SAUCE.

Spicy Sauce
2 tablespoons oyster sauce
2 tablespoons soy sauce
2 tablespoons water
1 tablespoon white vinegar
1 tablespoon sugar
1 teaspoon sambal oelek chili paste
½ teaspoon Koon Chun ground bean sauce, or a brand of your choice
½ teaspoon Asian sesame oil

1 cup canola oil
1 pound eggplant, peeled and cut into 1-inch cubes
1 teaspoon minced garlic
2 or 3 green onions, sliced
1 tablespoon cornstarch

1. Do ahead: To make the spicy sauce, whisk together all the sauce ingredients and set aside or refrigerate, covered, until ready to use.

2. Heat the canola oil to 375°F in a wok or deep-fryer. Working in batches, fry the eggplant until light brown, then drain on paper towels. Eggplant will soak up a lot of oil, so cook over high heat to get it fried quickly.

3. If you are using a wok, discard all but 1½ teaspoons of the oil and stir-fry the garlic and green onions until the garlic is soft. Add the sauce and let the mixture simmer for 2 minutes.

4. Return the eggplant to the pan and simmer for a few minutes more. Mix the cornstarch with 2 tablespoons water and whisk into the wok, then let the sauce simmer until thickened. Transfer to a platter and serve.

Serves 3 to 4

AT-HOME COST: $5

Look for the sambal oelek and ground bean sauce in the international section of your market.

Once you master the recipe, try substituting other vegetables, such as broccoli and cauliflower.

PONDEROSA STEAKHOUSE

seafood penne pasta salad

PENNE PASTA TOSSED WITH FRESH CRAB AND VEGETABLES IN A CREAMY SOUR
CREAM–RANCH DRESSING. PERFECT FOR A LUNCH ENTRÉE!

2 cups sour cream
2 cups ranch dressing, homemade
   or store-bought
¼ cup milk
1½ pounds penne pasta, cooked
   according to the package
   directions and chilled

½ cup chopped onion
½ cup chopped green bell pepper
½ cup chopped celery
1 pound crabmeat, imitation or
   fresh

1. Do ahead: Combine the sour cream, ranch dressing, and milk and whisk
   well to thoroughly combine. Cover and refrigerate for at least 2 hours
   before it's needed.

2. Put the chilled penne in a bowl and add the onion, bell pepper, celery,
   and crabmeat. Spoon the dressing over the mixture and stir to combine
   the ingredients well.

3. Cover the bowl and chill the salad for at least 2 hours before serving.

Serves 4

AT-HOME COST: $7.50

Ponderosa Steakhouse started out as a single restaurant in 1965 and
has evolved into one of the largest steakhouse chains in the world,
with more than two hundred Old West–styled restaurants.

RADISSON INN

roasted sicilian pork shoulder

RICHLY SEASONED PORK SHOULDER, SLOWLY ROASTED WITH A SAUSAGE, FONTINA, AND SPINACH STUFFING.

2 tablespoons minced garlic
3 tablespoons chopped shallots
3 tablespoons olive oil
8 ounces bulk Italian sausage
1 cup shredded fresh basil leaves
½ cup pine nuts

1 cup shredded Fontina cheese
Kosher salt and black pepper
2 tablespoons dried basil
2 tablespoons minced garlic
1½ teaspoons red pepper flakes
2 tablespoons olive oil

Roast
One 3-pound boneless pork shoulder, butterflied (have your butcher do this)
2 cups spinach, blanched

Special Equipment
Kitchen twine, cut into 12 pieces long enough to wrap around the roast

1. Sauté the garlic and shallots in the 3 tablespoons olive oil until translucent. Add the Italian sausage, breaking it up as it cooks. When the sausage is cooked all the way through, add the basil and pine nuts. Mix the ingredients well and set aside.

2. Preheat the oven to 350°F.

3. Lay the roast on a work surface with the inside facing up and spread the sautéed sausage mixture over the meat. Cover with the blanched spinach, then sprinkle the spinach with the Fontina. Season with salt and pepper.

4. Starting with one of the long sides, roll up the roast like a jelly roll and tie with the pieces of twine at 2-inch intervals, until it is firmly rolled.

5. Place the roast, seam side down, in a roasting pan and sprinkle with 2 tablespoons salt, 2 tablespoons black pepper, the basil, garlic, and red pepper flakes. Drizzle the olive oil over the whole roast. Bake for about 1 hour, or until the pork has formed a crust over the top and the internal temperature is between 165° and 170°F. Let the roast sit for 5 minutes, then cut the twine with a sharp knife or scissors and carve the roast.

Serves 10

While letting the roast sit, pour off the fat from the roasting pan and deglaze with ¼ cup white wine or water. Put the roasting pan over low heat and start scraping up all the browned bits into the wine and cooking juices. Mix 1 teaspoon of cornstarch with 2 tablespoons of water and whisk into the simmering liquid. Taste for seasoning and serve with the pork roast. If you really like the taste of fresh herbs, such as rosemary and thyme, tuck a sprig of one or more under the twine and let the flavor seep into the meat.

RED LOBSTER
amarillo salmon

BROILED SALMON FILLETS WITH A HOT AND SPICY BARBECUE SAUCE THAT'S EASY
TO MAKE AHEAD.

½ cup thick and spicy barbecue
sauce, homemade or store-
bought

¼ cup prepared horseradish sauce
Four 8-ounce salmon fillets
Salt and pepper

1. Do ahead: Combine the barbecue sauce and the horseradish sauce and
    mix well. Keep covered in the refrigerator until ready to use.
2. Preheat the broiler and line a broiler pan with foil. (Or you might want
    to light a charcoal grill.)
3. Season the salmon with salt and pepper and broil, turning once, until
    the salmon is cooked through. Lightly baste both sides of the fish with
    the sauce as it's cooking.
4. Plate the salmon and serve with extra sauce on the side.

Serves 4

AT-HOME COST: $9.50

In 1968, Bill Darden opened the first Red Lobster in Lakeland,
Florida. By the early 1970s, the company had expanded throughout
the southeast United States, making Red Lobster the leader in
seafood and casual dining. The chain continues to grow and today
has more than 680 restaurants.

RED LOBSTER
broiled dill salmon

BROILED SALMON LIGHTLY GLAZED WITH A LEMON-DILL SAUCE.

8 tablespoons (1 stick) butter
2 teaspoons lemon juice
1 tablespoon chopped fresh dill,
   or 1 teaspoon dried
Pinch of red pepper flakes

Four 8-ounce salmon steaks
   (1 inch thick)
1 teaspoon kosher salt
1 teaspoon black pepper

1. Melt the butter and add the lemon juice, dill, and red pepper flakes.
2. Preheat the broiler and line a broiler pan with foil.
3. Season the salmon with the salt and black pepper. Reserve some of the sauce for serving, then lightly baste with the remaining sauce.
4. Broil, turning once, until the fish is cooked through, basting both sides with the sauce.
5. Plate the salmon and serve with the warmed reserved sauce on the side.

Serves 4

AT-HOME COST: $8.50

You can also use ½ cup olive oil, or half butter and half olive oil, for the sauce. If dill is not your favorite, try substituting minced fresh parsley or thyme.

RED LOBSTER
country fried flounder

FLAKY WHITE-FLESHED FLOUNDER, DEEP-FRIED IN A DELICATE BUTTERMILK
AND CORNMEAL BATTER.

2 pounds flounder fillets
1 cup buttermilk
1 cup cornmeal
1/2 cup self-rising flour
1 teaspoon salt

1/2 teaspoon paprika
1/2 teaspoon pepper
2 cups vegetable oil, for frying
2 lemons, quartered

1. Do ahead: Cut the fillets into 6 even portions. Put them in a shallow bowl or container and cover with the buttermilk. Cover and refrigerate for 1 hour.

2. Combine the cornmeal and flour with the salt and spices and whisk to mix well. Dip the drained fillets into the cornmeal mixture and press down, making sure to coat both sides. Lay out on a plate and refrigerate for 30 minutes.

3. Heat the vegetable oil in a skillet and fry the fish, turning once, until golden brown on both sides. Drain on paper towels.

4. Serve each portion on a warmed plate with a lemon quarter.

Serves 6

AT-HOME COST: $8.00

If fresh flounder is not available, try substituting tilapia, snapper, whitefish, or halibut.

Refrigerating coated fillets for 30 minutes before cooking lets the wet and dry ingredients solidify enough to stay on the fish during frying.

RED LOBSTER
crab linguine alfredo

SWEET CRABMEAT TOSSED IN A PARMESAN CREAM SAUCE WITH LINGUINE. A
PINCH OF CAYENNE PEPPER GIVES THIS DISH A LITTLE EXTRA ZIP.

1 teaspoon butter
1 teaspoon all-purpose flour
½ cup half-and-half, plus more as needed
6 ounces snow crab meat, cut into chunks
3 tablespoons grated Parmesan cheese, plus extra for serving

Salt and white pepper
Pinch of cayenne pepper
4 ounces linguine pasta, cooked according to the package directions

1. In a small saucepan, melt the butter and whisk in the flour, stirring constantly, until the mixture is smooth. Add the half-and-half and simmer for about 5 minutes.

2. Add the crabmeat and the 3 tablespoons Parmesan and stir to combine well. Season with salt and white pepper and a pinch of cayenne. Stir and let simmer for 2 minutes. If the sauce gets too thick, thin it with a little more half-and-half.

3. Toss the cooked pasta with the crab sauce. Serve the pasta in a warmed bowl and finish with a little more Parmesan cheese.

Serves 1

AT-HOME COST: $9.50

Many other types of crab are available. Try Alaska king crab for a similar sweetness and texture.

RED LOBSTER
crab-stuffed mushrooms

TENDER BUTTON MUSHROOMS STUFFED WITH CRACKERS AND FRESH CRAB, TRADITIONAL SPICES, AND PARMESAN CHEESE, BAKED UNTIL BUBBLY AND GOLDEN BROWN.

1 pound button mushrooms
(35 to 40)
2 tablespoons butter
1/4 cup finely chopped celery
2 tablespoons finely chopped
onion
2 tablespoons finely chopped red
bell pepper
8 ounces crab claw meat
2 cups crushed oyster crackers

1/2 cup shredded Parmesan
cheese
1/4 teaspoon garlic powder
1 teaspoon dried parsley
1/2 teaspoon Old Bay Seasoning
1/4 teaspoon pepper
1/4 teaspoon kosher salt
1 large egg, beaten
6 ounces Parmesan cheese, grated
Minced fresh parsley, for topping

1. Do ahead: Remove the stems from the mushrooms and finely chop about half of them. Save the remainder of the stems for another use. Reserve the caps.

2. Melt the butter and sauté the mushroom stems, celery, onion, and bell pepper. When the vegetables are soft, add the crabmeat and the crushed crackers. Continue to sauté until most of the liquid has been absorbed by the crackers. Set aside to cool.

3. Preheat the oven to 400°F.

4. Combine the cooled crab mixture with the shredded Parmesan, garlic powder, parsley, spices, salt, and the beaten egg. Stuff each mushroom cap with a teaspoon of the mixture.

5. Put the filled caps in a baking dish large enough to hold them in a single layer. Carefully add 1/2 cup of water to the pan. Sprinkle the grated Parmesan over the mushrooms and bake for about 15 minutes, or until the mushrooms are cooked through and golden brown.

AT-HOME COST: $7

For individual servings, bake the stuffed caps in individual small casserole dishes.

There are many types of crabmeat available, from Dungeness on the Pacific coast to jumbo lump on the Atlantic coast.

This might be the time to use imitation crab, called surimi.

RED LOBSTER
cranberry-apple sangria

A REFRESHING BLEND OF WINE, LIQUOR, AND FRUIT JUICE GARNISHED WITH
FRESH FRUIT.

2 tablespoons whole berry cranberry sauce, with juice	2 tablespoons cranberry juice cocktail
1½ teaspoons Sour Apple Pucker schnapps	1 tablespoon orange juice
1½ teaspoons Triple Sec	¾ cup chardonnay
1 tablespoon Tuaca liqueur	¾ cup white zinfandel
	Orange wedges and green apple chunks, for garnish

1. Put the cranberry sauce, Sour Apple Pucker, Triple Sec, Tuaca, cranberry juice cocktail, and orange juice in a blender and process for about 5 seconds, until the cranberries are chopped but not pureed.

2. Add the chardonnay and white zinfandel, mix well by hand, and pour over ice into 2 large glasses.

3. Skewer some orange and apple pieces onto 2 toothpicks and garnish each drink.

Serves 2

AT-HOME COST: $9.75

You can substitute any dry white wine for the chardonnay.

Tuaca is an Italian liqueur flavored with citrus and vanilla. You may want to substitute Grand Marnier, Cointreau, or additional Triple Sec.

RED LOBSTER
mussels marinara

FRESH MUSSELS SIMMERED IN A TOMATO-HERB BROTH AND SERVED OVER ANGEL HAIR PASTA.

1 cup dry white wine or chicken broth

2 tablespoons chopped fresh garlic, or 2 teaspoons granulated

2 tablespoons chopped fresh basil, or 2 teaspoons dried

2 tablespoons chopped fresh parsley, or 2 teaspoons parsley flakes

1 teaspoon dried marjoram

1/2 teaspoon dried oregano

24 black mussels, debearded and scrubbed

1/4 cup minced onion

1 cup diced tomatoes

1 teaspoon kosher salt

1/4 teaspoon white pepper

1 tablespoon cornstarch

12 ounces angel hair pasta, cooked according to the package directions

1. In a stockpot, simmer the wine with the garlic, basil, and parsley, then add the marjoram and oregano. Stir once to blend all the ingredients.

2. Add the mussels to the pot along with the onion and tomatoes. Cover and let simmer until the mussels open, about 8 minutes. Discard any that don't open.

3. Season the broth with salt and white pepper, then add the cornstarch and whisk until slightly thickened. Plate the warm pasta and serve with the mussels and sauce on top.

Serves 2 to 4

AT-HOME COST: $9

Use half wine and half clam juice or chicken broth to steam the mussels for a mellower flavor. Use another type of pasta if you like—spaghettini would be a good choice.

Mussels are raised in very cold water and found in almost every region of the world.

RED LOBSTER
seafood chili

PERFECTLY SEASONED CHILI MADE WITH CLAMS, MUSSELS, FISH, SHRIMP, AND SCALLOPS.

Chili
4 teaspoons cumin seeds

¼ cup olive oil or vegetable oil

2 cups chopped onions

2 leeks, white parts only, trimmed

1 large rib celery, chopped

8 cloves garlic, minced

3 tablespoons minced celery leaves

5 teaspoons dried oregano

Two 15-ounce cans plum tomatoes, chopped, with juice

2 tablespoons tomato paste

2 cups clam juice

2 cups dry red wine

½ cup chili garlic paste

1 medium red bell pepper, chopped

1 teaspoon cayenne pepper

1 teaspoon salt

Seafood
8 littleneck clams

8 mussels, debearded and scrubbed

1 pound cod, cut into bite-size pieces

8 large shrimp, peeled and deveined

¾ pound bay scallops

½ cup minced fresh parsley, for garnish

1. Do ahead: Make the chili the day before you want to serve it—add the seafood the next day.

2. Do ahead: Toast the cumin seeds in a small skillet over medium heat until they begin to release their aroma. Let cool and set aside until ready to use.

3. Heat the oil in a large saucepan and sauté the onions, leeks, and celery until soft. Add the garlic and sauté for about 1 minute, then add the celery leaves, dried oregano, and chopped tomatoes. Let the mixture simmer for 5 minutes.

4. Mix the tomato paste with the clam juice and red wine, then add to the saucepan and simmer for 5 minutes. Finally, add the chili garlic

paste, toasted cumin seeds, bell pepper, and cayenne. Season with the 1 teaspoon salt and stir. Simmer for 10 minutes. Let the chili cool, then put it in a covered container and refrigerate overnight.

5. The next day, put the chili in a large saucepan and slowly bring it to a low boil. First add the clams and cover the pan; simmer for 5 minutes. Add the mussels, cover the pan, and simmer for 5 minutes. Stir in the cod and shrimp, cover, and simmer for 3 to 5 minutes. Last, stir in the bay scallops, which will take only a few moments to cook through. Discard any mussels or clams that do not open.

6. Ladle into warmed bowls and garnish with parsley.

Serves 4

AT-HOME COST: $10

Substitute another firm white fish if the cod is not available. Halibut or snapper would be a good choice.

RED LOBSTER
shrimp scampi

SAUTÉED SHRIMP IN A CLASSIC WHITE WINE–GARLIC SAUCE.

1 cup white wine
3 tablespoons minced garlic
1 pound medium shrimp, peeled and deveined
8 tablespoons (1 stick) unsalted butter, cut into chunks

Salt and pepper
1 tablespoon chopped fresh parsley, for garnish

1. Heat a skillet and add the wine and garlic. Let the wine reduce by half. The garlic should be soft.

2. When the wine is reduced, add the shrimp and stir until they are almost pink all the way through. Lower the heat.

3. Start whisking in the butter a piece at a time until it is all incorporated and the sauce has emulsified. Season with salt and pepper and garnish with the parsley.

Serves 2 to 4

AT-HOME COST: $8.50

RED ROBIN

banzai burger

FRESHLY GROUND BEEF MARINATED IN TERIYAKI SAUCE AND TOPPED WITH
GRILLED PINEAPPLE AND CHEDDAR CHEESE.

¼ cup teriyaki sauce
One 5-ounce ground beef
  patty
1 canned pineapple ring
2 slices Cheddar cheese

1 sesame seed hamburger bun,
  split in half
1 tablespoon mayonnaise
¼ cup shredded lettuce
2 tomato slices

1. Do ahead: Pour the teriyaki sauce into a shallow bowl and add the patty, turning to coat both sides. Refrigerate for 30 minutes.

2. Grill or sear the patty until cooked to your preferred doneness, turning once. Remove the patty from the grill and keep warm.

3. Sear or broil the pineapple ring, turning once, until there is some charring on each side. Put the pineapple ring on the cooked patty and top with the Cheddar cheese.

4. Toast the hamburger bun, then spread the top and bottom halves with the mayonnaise. Place the patty on the bottom half of the bun and garnish with the shredded lettuce and the tomato slices. Cover with the top half and serve.

Serves 1

AT-HOME COST: $5.50

Red Robin Gourmet Burgers first opened their doors in Seattle, Washington, in 1969. Their focus is on serving an imaginative selection of high-quality gourmet burgers in a family-friendly atmosphere.

RED ROBIN
bbq chicken salad

CRISP GREENS TOPPED WITH TOMATO, BARBECUED CHICKEN, BLACK BEANS, CHEESE, BACON, SLICED AVOCADO, AND CRUNCHY FRENCH-FRIED ONIONS. SERVED WITH RANCH DRESSING.

1 cup chopped romaine lettuce
1 cup chopped iceberg lettuce
½ cup chopped red cabbage
½ cup refried black beans
1 boneless, skinless chicken breast
½ cup barbecue sauce, such as
   Bull's-Eye or KC Masterpiece
¼ cup chopped tomato

½ cup shredded Cheddar cheese
¼ cup French's French Fried
   Onions
2 slices bacon, cooked and drained,
   crumbled
¼ avocado, sliced
¼ cup ranch dressing, for serving

1. Do ahead: Combine the 2 lettuces with the cabbage. Heat the refried beans.

2. Preheat the grill or broiler.

3. Grill the chicken breast, basting with the barbecue sauce on both sides. When cooked through and no longer pink in the middle, let it cool, then slice into bite-size pieces.

3. Spread the lettuces and cabbage on the bottom of a plate. Cover with the chopped tomato. Spread the warm beans over the tomatoes on one side of the plate, and put the sliced chicken over the tomatoes on the other side of the plate.

4. Sprinkle the whole plate with the shredded Cheddar, then the fried onion rings, and then the crumbled bacon. Finish with the slices of avocado. Serve with ranch dressing on the side.

Serves 1

AT-HOME COST: $7.00

If you don't want to buy barbecue sauce, try using some of the recipes in this book—they can yield more than is necessary for a single recipe.

Use tortilla strips instead of the canned fried onion rings; they will provide the needed crunch.

RED ROBIN
burnin' love burger

YOU'LL GET FIRED UP FOR THE JALAPEÑO RINGS, TANGY SALSA, AND SPICY PEPPER JACK CHEESE LAYERED ON TOP OF THIS CAYENNE-SEASONED BEEF BURGER. IT'S TOPPED WITH SHREDDED LETTUCE AND TOMATO TO COOL THINGS OFF AND SERVED ON A JALAPEÑO-CORNMEAL KAISER ROLL WITH CHIPOTLE MAYO.

Red Robin Seasoning Salt
3 tablespoons salt
1 tablespoon instant tomato soup mix
2 teaspoons chili powder
¼ teaspoon ground cumin
¼ teaspoon pepper

Chipotle Mayonnaise
¼ cup mayonnaise
¼ teaspoon mashed chipotle pepper
Pinch of paprika

Burger
1 jalapeño-cornmeal kaiser roll or sesame seed hamburger bun, split in half
One 5-ounce ground beef patty
2 slices pepper Jack cheese
2 tablespoons fresh salsa or pico de gallo (page 16 or 70) or store-bought salsa
1 jalapeño pepper, cut into 4 to 6 slices
⅓ cup shredded iceberg lettuce
Sliced tomato

1. Do ahead: Combine all the ingredients for the seasoning salt and set aside or store in a covered container until ready to use.

2. Do ahead: Make the chipotle mayonnaise by carefully whisking all the ingredients together. Make sure the chipotle is mashed up well enough to be completely incorporated.

3. Preheat the grill or the broiler.

4. Toast the roll and set aside. Season both sides of the patty with ¼ teaspoon of the seasoning salt. Grill or broil, turning once, until cooked to your desired doneness. Add the pepper Jack cheese to the patty while it still has a few minutes left to cook so that the cheese melts.

5. Assemble the burger: Spread the chipotle mayonnaise on the top and bottom halves of the bun. Put the cooked patty on the bottom half and

top with the salsa, jalapeño slices, shredded lettuce, and 1 or 2 slices of tomato. Cover with the top half of the bun and serve.

Serves 1

AT-HOME COST: $3.00

RUBY TUESDAY

spicy sesame-peanut noodles

SPAGHETTI TOSSED WITH ASIAN-STYLE PEANUT SAUCE AND TOPPED WITH GREEN
ONIONS AND SESAME SEEDS.

2 teaspoons sesame seeds,
for garnish
¾ cup chunky-style peanut
butter
¼ cup chicken broth or water
2 teaspoons grated peeled fresh
ginger
2 cloves garlic, chopped

½ teaspoon salt
¼ teaspoon red pepper flakes
8 ounces spaghetti, cooked
according to the package
directions
2 tablespoons Asian sesame oil
2 green onions, thinly sliced, for
garnish

1. Do ahead: Toast the sesame seeds in a small skillet over medium heat.
   They should just start to turn very light brown and release a sesame
   aroma. Let cool and set aside or keep in a covered container until ready
   to use.

2. Combine the peanut butter, broth, ginger, garlic, salt, and red pepper
   flakes in a blender and process until combined, but not pureed—the
   mixture should still be a little chunky.

3. Toss the cooked pasta with the sauce and refrigerate, covered, for at least
   1 hour.

4. When ready to serve, drizzle the pasta with the sesame oil and stir to
   blend. Plate the noodles on a platter and garnish with the green onions
   and sesame seeds.

Serves 2

AT-HOME COST: $6

Use different noodles if you like. Vermicelli and spaghettini would be good alternatives. You might also try Asian noodles, such as ramen or soba.

Ruby Tuesday got its start in 1972, when Sandy Beall and four of his fraternity buddies from the University of Tennessee established the first restaurant adjacent to the college campus in Knoxville. Today, Ruby Tuesday is one of three large public companies that dominate the bar-and-grill category of casual dining.

RUTH'S CHRIS STEAK HOUSE
creamed spinach

THE CLASSIC NEW ORLEANS VERSION, QUICKLY FINISHED UNDER A BROILER TO LIGHTLY BROWN THE SAUCE.

Béchamel Sauce
8 tablespoons (1 stick) butter
¼ cup all-purpose flour
2 tablespoons chopped onion
1 clove garlic, chopped
2 cups milk

1 bay leaf
Salt and pepper

1 pound fresh spinach, cleaned and stemmed
2 tablespoons butter, softened

1. Do ahead: To make the béchamel sauce, in a medium saucepan, melt the 8 tablespoons butter over medium heat. Whisk in the flour, stirring constantly, until the paste is smooth and very slightly browned. Add the onion and garlic, whisking for a minute or two. Gradually add the milk and lower the heat to a simmer. Stir to blend well. Add the bay leaf and season with salt and pepper. Simmer for 5 minutes.

2. Lightly blanch the spinach and dry in hand towels or paper towels—the spinach must be very dry. Put it in a blender and process it to a puree.

3. Strain the béchamel sauce and stir in the pureed spinach, then add the 2 tablespoons softened butter. To finish it restaurant style, put it in an ovenproof baking dish and run it under the broiler for a few moments, until the sauce begins to bubble and turn golden brown.

Serves 4

AT-HOME COST: $3.50

To make a classic béchamel, add a pinch of freshly grated nutmeg.

This international chain is famous for its signature steaks—seared to perfection and topped with fresh butter so that they sizzle all the way to your table. The food is delicious, but be careful not to touch the plate—it comes out super hot! They usually warn you in advance, but I still had to learn this the hard way. However, serving your cooked steak on a heated plate is a good idea: it keeps the steak warm and juicy while you're eating it.

SARA LEE

carrot square cake

THE OLD-FASHIONED GOODNESS OF CREAM CHEESE–FROSTED CARROT CAKE
STUDDED WITH RAISINS AND WALNUTS.

Cream Cheese Frosting
6 ounces cream cheese, softened
8 tablespoons (½ cup) butter, softened
1 pound confectioners' sugar
1½ teaspoons orange extract
1 teaspoon grated orange zest

Cake
2 eggs, beaten
1 teaspoon vanilla extract
¾ cup vegetable oil

1 teaspoon salt
1½ teaspoons baking powder
2 teaspoons ground cinnamon
1 cup sugar
1¼ cups all-purpose flour, plus extra for the pan
1 cup finely grated carrots
1 cup chopped walnuts, plus extra for garnish (optional)
½ cup golden raisins (optional)

1. Do ahead: Make the cream cheese frosting: Beat together the cream cheese and butter, using an electric mixer at high speed, until fluffy. Lower the speed to medium and add half the confectioners' sugar, then increase the speed back to high and add the orange extract and the orange zest. Beat for 1 minute. Reduce the speed to medium and add the remaining confectioners' sugar. Set aside until ready to use. If you refrigerate the frosting until later, you will need to let it come back up to room temperature before applying it to the cake.

2. Preheat the oven to 325°F. Grease and flour a 9-inch square pan.

3. Combine the eggs with the vanilla extract, vegetable oil, salt, baking powder, cinnamon, sugar, and flour. Beat with an electric mixer for 3 minutes on medium-high speed. Stir in the carrots, the 1 cup walnuts, and the raisins, if desired. Spread the batter evenly in the prepared pan and bake for 45 to 50 minutes, until a toothpick inserted in the center comes out clean.

4. Let the cake cool completely on a rack before frosting. Remove from the pan and spread the frosting on the top and sides of the cake; sprinkle on some of the reserved walnuts, if desired. Store in the refrigerator.

Serves 6

AT-HOME COST: $6.50

If you can't find orange extract, use vanilla extract and a teaspoon of grated lemon zest.

The Sara Lee bakery produces a line of cakes, desserts, and pastries made to the highest possible standard using the finest ingredients, whatever the cost and without the use of artificial colors, flavorings, or preservatives.

SBARRO

chicken francese with lemon butter

CHICKEN BREASTS, ROMANO CHEESE, MUSHROOMS, AND SBARRO'S SIGNATURE FRANCESE SAUCE.

5 eggs

¼ cup plus 2 tablespoons grated Romano cheese

1 teaspoon parsley flakes

1 cup all-purpose flour

Five 5-ounce boneless, skinless chicken breasts, pounded ¼ inch thick

1⅓ cups vegetable oil

2 tablespoons olive oil

1 cup chicken broth

Juice from 2 lemons

½ pound (2 sticks) butter, cut into pieces

Salt and white pepper

Chopped fresh parsley, for garnish

Lemon slices, for garnish

1. Beat the eggs and add the cheese and parsley flakes. Put the flour in a shallow bowl. Dip the chicken in the flour, then in the egg mixture, then in the flour again.

2. Heat the vegetable oil and the olive oil in a skillet and fry the chicken until golden on both sides, turning once. Drain on paper towels and keep warm. Pour off most of the oil and sauté the mushrooms over medium heat until browned. Remove from the pan and set aside.

3. Discard any remaining oil and add the chicken broth to the skillet. Bring to a boil and reduce by half, making sure to scrape up any browned bits left from the chicken. Add the lemon juice, then the butter, whisking constantly until it is melted. Return the mushrooms to the pan. Season with salt and white pepper.

4. Plate the chicken breasts and pour the sauce over. Garnish with the chopped parsley and the lemon slices.

Serves 5

AT-HOME COST: $7

Sbarro opened in 1956, selling fresh food and authentic Italian fare, including homemade mozzarella, imported cheeses, and delicious sausage and salami. In 1967, Sbarro opened its first mall-based restaurant selling authentic Italian food.

SBARRO

rigatoni alla vodka

CLASSIC ITALIAN PASTA IN A "PINK" SAUCE, A COMBINATION OF TOMATO SAUCE, CREAM, AND VODKA.

2 tablespoons olive oil
2 cloves garlic, minced
One 24-ounce can tomato
  sauce
½ teaspoon whole pink
  peppercorns, cracked
1 tablespoon salt
½ teaspoon black pepper
1 teaspoon dried basil
2 cups heavy cream
3 tablespoons vodka

2 pounds rigatoni pasta, cooked
  according to the package
  directions

Garnish
3 tablespoons grated Romano
  cheese
3 tablespoons bacon bits or
  cooked, crumbled bacon
1½ tablespoons chopped fresh
  Italian parsley

1. Heat the olive oil in a medium saucepan and sauté the garlic until translucent. Add the tomato sauce and the cracked pink peppercorns. Season with the salt and black pepper, then add the dried basil. Simmer for 10 minutes over low heat.

2. Whisk in the heavy cream and the vodka. Simmer for 5 minutes, or until the sauce is slightly thickened.

3. Toss with the rigatoni and garnish with the Romano cheese, bacon, and parsley.

Serves 8

AT-HOME COST: $7.50

Substitute another pasta, such as penne or mostaccioli, if you prefer.

SHONEY'S
country fried steak

TENDER BEEFSTEAK LIGHTLY BREADED IN SEASONED FLOUR, THEN FRIED AND SMOTHERED IN HOT COUNTRY GRAVY.

2 cups all-purpose flour
2 teaspoons salt
¼ teaspoon pepper
Four 4-ounce cube steaks

Gravy
1 tablespoon vegetable oil
1½ tablespoons lean ground beef (see Note)

¼ cup all-purpose flour
¼ teaspoon salt
¼ teaspoon pepper
2 cups chicken broth
2 cups milk

2 cups vegetable oil, for frying

1. Do ahead: Combine the 2 cups flour with the salt and pepper. Put some water in a shallow bowl. Dip the steaks in the water, then in the flour mixture. Line a plate or baking sheet with waxed paper and put each steak on it. Freeze the steaks for 3 hours.

2. Do ahead: Make the gravy in a small saucepan: Heat the 1 tablespoon oil and sauté the ground beef, breaking it up as it cooks. Whisk in the ¼ cup flour and stir until the paste is smooth. Season with the salt and pepper, then add the chicken broth and milk. Bring to a boil, then lower the heat and simmer for 10 minutes. The sauce should be slightly thickened.

3. Heat the 2 cups vegetable oil in a heavy skillet and bring the temperature up to 350°F. Fry the frozen cube steaks, one at a time, until they are golden brown on each side, turning once. Drain and keep warm.

4. Plate the steaks and pour the warm gravy over each serving.

Note: If you don't want to buy a small amount of ground beef, trim a little off each of the steaks and mince it until you have your 1½ tablespoons meat.

AT-HOME COST: $8

Shoney's started as a drive-in restaurant called Parkette in Charleston, West Virginia, in 1947. It acquired a Big Boy franchise in 1951 and was renamed the Parkette Shoney's Big Boy in 1953. By 1972, Big Boy was dropped from the name. Shoney's presently has more than 1,300 restaurants that offer a full-service casual dining experience and a menu consisting of home-style cuisine.

SHONEY'S
chicken stir-fry

STIR-FRIED CHICKEN, MUSHROOMS, ONION, BROCCOLI, CARROTS, AND GREEN
BELL PEPPER SERVED OVER CHICKEN-FLAVORED RICE.

6 ounces boneless, skinless chicken
breast, cut into pieces
½ cup plus 2 tablespoons teriyaki
sauce
2 tablespoons vegetable oil
3 mushrooms, sliced
¼ onion, cut into thin wedges
¼ cup broccoli florets

¼ cup shredded carrot
¼ cup thinly sliced green bell
pepper
White rice, cooked according to
the package directions but
substituting chicken broth for
the water, for serving (optional)

1. Do ahead: Marinate the chicken pieces in ¼ cup of the teriyaki sauce for
   at least 2 hours in the refrigerator.

2. Heat the oil in a wok or skillet and sauté the chicken pieces until cooked
   through. Discard the marinade. Add the mushrooms and the remaining
   ¼ cup plus 2 tablespoons teriyaki sauce and stir-fry for 1 minute. Add
   the onion, broccoli, carrot, and bell pepper. Cover the wok or skillet for
   a few minutes and lower the heat, simmering until the vegetables are
   tender.

3. Take the cover off the pan and finish stir-frying the ingredients. Serve
   with white rice, if desired.

Serves 1

AT-HOME COST: $5

SONIC DRIVE-IN
fritos chili cheese wraps

GET A HEARTY HELPING OF WARM CHILI, MELTED CHEESE, AND FRITOS CORN
CHIPS—ALL WRAPPED UP IN A WARM FLOUR TORTILLA.

One 19-ounce can mild chili
3 cups Fritos or other corn chips
   (original style)
Four 10-inch flour tortillas

1 cup shredded mild Cheddar
   cheese
¼ to ½ cup diced onion

1. Combine the chili and Fritos in a large bowl. Fill the center of a flour tortilla with one-fourth of the mixture and top with ¼ cup of the Cheddar and 1 or 2 tablespoons of the onion.

2. Fold in 2 sides and roll up the tortilla. Heat in a microwave for about 15 seconds, until the mixture is hot. Repeat with the remaining ingredients to make 3 more wraps.

Serves 4

AT-HOME COST: $5

Kick it up a notch by using a spicier chili or by adding red pepper flakes and cayenne to taste.

Sonic is the largest chain of drive-in restaurants. Serving made-to-order American classics and signature menu items, Sonic offers speedy service from friendly carhops as well as heaped helpings of fun and personality.

STARBUCKS
tazo chai tea latte

A SPICY DRINK OF BLACK TEA INFUSED WITH CARDAMOM, CINNAMON, BLACK PEPPER, AND STAR ANISE ADDED TO FRESHLY STEAMED MILK.

6 to 8 green cardamom pods
2 whole black peppercorns
1 or 2 slices peeled fresh ginger, diced
2 sticks cinnamon

1 or 2 whole cloves
2/3 cup milk
4 teaspoons honey
2 to 3 teaspoons loose black tea

1. In a medium saucepan, bring 2½ cups water to a boil along with the cardamom, peppercorns, ginger, cinnamon, and cloves. Reduce the heat and simmer for 10 minutes.

2. Stir in the milk and honey. Continue stirring until the honey is dissolved. Bring to a low boil and add the loose tea. Remove the pan from the heat and let sit for 5 minutes.

3. Strain the solids from the latte and pour into 2 cups. Serve hot.

Serves 2

AT-HOME COST: $2.00

Starbucks was founded in 1971 in Seattle, Washington, and has since risen to be the largest coffeehouse in the world. They offer more than thirty kinds of coffee as well as other drinks, foods, and merchandise.

STEAK AND ALE
bourbon street steak

NEW YORK STRIP STEAK MARINATED IN BOURBON AND BROWN SUGAR. SERVE
WITH STEAK AND ALE BURGUNDY MUSHROOMS (OPPOSITE).

1½ teaspoons diced onion
3 tablespoons bourbon
3 tablespoons soy sauce
3 tablespoons packed dark
  brown sugar

3 tablespoons lemon juice
1 clove garlic, chopped
One 10-ounce New York strip
  steak

1. Do ahead: Combine all the ingredients except the steak and whisk
   together. Pour the marinade into a container and add the steak. Cover
   the container and marinate the meat for 4 hours, turning every
   30 minutes.

2. Preheat the grill or the broiler. Remove the steak from the marinade and
   grill or broil it to your desired doneness. Discard the marinade.

Serves 1

AT-HOME COST: $6.50

You can use any whiskey or bourbon you prefer or substitute brandy
or dry sherry.

Steak and Ale first opened in Dallas, Texas, in 1966 and grew into
one of the top chain steakhouses in the late 1980s.

STEAK AND ALE

burgundy mushrooms

MUSHROOMS IN A BURGUNDY WINE SAUCE.

2 tablespoons butter
¾ cup diced onion
½ cup dry red wine
¼ teaspoon garlic powder
¼ teaspoon ground white pepper

2 beef bouillon cubes
¼ cup lemon juice
1¼ pounds portobello
  mushrooms, cleaned and dried,
  whole or chopped

1. Heat the butter in a skillet and sauté the onion until soft, but not browned.

2. In a bowl, combine the wine, garlic powder, white pepper, and beef bouillon cubes and whisk until the cubes are dissolved. Add this mixture to the skillet with the onion and simmer for about 10 minutes.

3. In a saucepan, boil 8 cups water and the lemon juice, then add the mushrooms and cook until they are slightly soft. Drain the mushrooms and add them to the onion-and-wine sauce, stirring well to coat. Heat through and serve with Bourbon Street Steak (opposite).

Serves 4

AT-HOME COST: $5

Steak and Ale opened in Dallas, Texas, in 1966. Pillsbury purchased it in 1976, then spun it off in 1982 to the S&A Restaurant Corp. In the late 1980s Steak and Ale was one of the top steakhouse chains, with more than 280 restaurants. Their success inspired the creation of similar chains, and competition eventually forced the chain out of business. It closed in July 2008 due to bankruptcy.

STEAK AND ALE

cajun chicken pasta

CAJUN-SEASONED CHICKEN BREAST SERVED ON TOP OF LINGUINE PASTA TOSSED WITH A CAJUN-SEASONED ALFREDO SAUCE—GARNISHED WITH TOMATO AND GREEN ONIONS. (IT'S GREAT SERVED WITH GARLIC BREAD.)

1 boneless, skinless chicken breast
1 tablespoon butter, melted
½ cup Cajun seasoning, homemade or store-bought
½ cup Alfredo sauce, homemade or store-bought

4 ounces linguine pasta, cooked according to the package directions

Garnish
1 tablespoon diced tomato
1 tablespoon sliced green onion

1. Dip the chicken breast into the melted butter and then into the Cajun seasoning.

2. Heat a cast-iron skillet until it is very hot—a drop of water should jump in the air when it hits the pan. Cook the chicken breast, turning once, until it is no longer pink in the middle. The pan will smoke as soon as the butter and seasoning hit the heat, but this is how food is "blackened."

3. Remove the chicken from the skillet and slice it. Warm the Alfredo sauce over low heat and toss with the linguine. Plate the pasta, put the chicken strips on top, and garnish with the tomato and green onion.

Serves 1

AT-HOME COST: $4

You'll find recipes in this book for Cajun seasoning and Alfredo sauce—homemade is always better!

If you use an Alfredo recipe that calls for grated cheese, save a little for the top of this dish.

If you don't have a cast-iron skillet, look in kitchen supply shops for an oval griddle with a handle (sometimes called a fajita pan). You can use it for blackening Cajun-style foods and for making fajitas.

STEAK AND ALE

hawaiian chicken

CHICKEN BREASTS MARINATED IN PINEAPPLE JUICE, SOY SAUCE, AND SHERRY, THEN GRILLED AND SERVED WITH RICE PILAF.

¼ cup soy sauce
½ cup dry sherry
1½ cups unsweetened pineapple juice
¼ cup red wine vinegar
¼ cup plus 2 tablespoons sugar
½ teaspoon garlic powder

4 to 6 boneless, skinless chicken breasts
1 slice Muenster or provolone cheese per chicken breast
Rice pilaf, homemade or store-bought, for serving (optional)

1. Do ahead: To make the marinade, combine the soy sauce, sherry, pineapple juice, vinegar, sugar, and garlic powder. Put the chicken in the marinade and cover and refrigerate overnight, turning occasionally.

2. Preheat the grill or the broiler. Line the broiler pan, if using, with foil. Remove the chicken from the marinade. Grill or broil the chicken, turning once, until cooked through (no longer pink in the middle). Baste with the marinade once on each uncooked side, then discard the marinade.

3. Just before the chicken is done, place a slice of cheese on top of each breast. Serve with rice pilaf, if you like.

Serves 4 to 6

AT-HOME COST: $9.75

TEXAS ROADHOUSE
smokehouse burgers

HALF-POUND CHUCK BURGERS WITH SAUTÉED MUSHROOMS, ONION, BARBECUE SAUCE, AND JACK AND CHEDDAR CHEESES, TOPPED WITH SHREDDED LETTUCE AND SLICED TOMATO.

Seasoned Pepper
1/3 cup whole black peppercorns
2 tablespoons sweet pepper flakes
2 tablespoons whole white peppercorns
1 teaspoon onion flakes
1 teaspoon red pepper flakes
1/2 teaspoon granulated garlic

8 slices Texas toast
2 tablespoons olive oil

4 ounces portobello mushrooms, sliced
1/4 cup sliced green onions
1 tablespoon roasted garlic
Four 8-ounce ground chuck patties
4 slices pepper Jack cheese
4 slices Cheddar cheese
1/2 cup shredded lettuce
1 medium tomato, thinly sliced
1/4 cup barbecue sauce, homemade or store-bought

1. Do ahead: To make the seasoned pepper, grind all the ingredients in a coffee or spice grinder until you have a coarsely ground powder. Set aside or store in a covered container until ready to use.

2. Preheat the grill or the broiler. Toast the slices of bread and keep warm.

3. Heat the olive oil in a skillet and add the sliced mushrooms. Sauté for 1 minute, then add the green onions and roasted garlic. Sauté for 1 minute, then set aside.

4. Sprinkle the patties with the seasoned pepper and grill or broil, turning once, until cooked to your preferred doneness. Just before the burgers are done, top each one with a slice each of pepper Jack and Cheddar and spoon on some of the sautéed mushrooms.

5. Put each burger on one of the toasted slices of bread and top with shredded lettuce and a tomato slice or two. Spread the top piece of toast with some of the barbecue sauce and assemble the sandwich.

AT-HOME COST: $8.50

Texas Toast can be found in the freezer section of large markets.

Substitute ground turkey or ground chicken patties for beef patties.

Serving large portions of hand-cut steaks, award-winning ribs, chicken dishes, fish, salads, and lots more, Texas Roadhouse can satisfy almost any appetite. Fresh-baked bread and made-from-scratch side items are the standard. Everything is created with only the highest-quality, freshest ingredients.

TEXAS ROADHOUSE

green beans

THE OLD-FASHIONED GOODNESS OF GREEN BEANS AND ONION WITH A HINT
OF BACON.

1 tablespoon sugar
½ teaspoon pepper
½ cup diced bacon

½ cup diced onion
2 pounds frozen green beans

1. In a small bowl, combine 2 cups water, the sugar, and the pepper. Whisk well and set aside.

2. Heat a skillet and cook the diced bacon. When it is almost completely cooked, add the onion and sauté until the onion is soft and slightly browned.

3. Add the sugar mixture to the bacon and onion, then add the green beans. Bring to a boil, then reduce the heat and simmer for 5 minutes, or until the beans are cooked. Serve hot.

Serves 4 to 6

AT-HOME COST: $4

TEXAS ROADHOUSE
grilled cheese wraps

CHEESE AND PEPPER IN EGG ROLL WRAPPERS, DEEP-FRIED, AND SERVED WITH MARINARA SAUCE.

8 slices Cheddar cheese
8 slices Monterey Jack cheese
1 jalapeño pepper, diced
1 teaspoon snipped fresh chives

Four 7-inch egg roll wrappers
1 large egg, beaten
2 cups vegetable oil, for frying
Marinara sauce, homemade or store-bought, for dipping

1. Do ahead: Build the cheese wraps. Place a slice of Cheddar on top of a slice of Jack and sprinkle with some of the diced jalapeño and chives. Top with another slice of Cheddar and Jack. Roll the cheese slices into a tight roll. Repeat with remaining cheese, diced pepper, and chives.

2. Place an egg roll wrapper on a work surface so that a pointed end is facing you. Place a cheese roll in the center and fold the left corner over the cheese. Brush the beaten egg on the tip of the right corner and fold the right corner over the cheese. Press the corners together so they will stick. Repeat the process with the top and bottom corners until you have enclosed the cheese roll in the wrapper. Make sure the wrap is well sealed, to prevent the filling from escaping during the frying.

3. Repeat with the remaining cheese rolls and wrappers, then refrigerate all the wraps for 30 minutes.

4. Heat the vegetable oil to 350°F in a wok or saucepan. Fry each roll until golden brown on all sides. Drain on paper towels and serve with warm marinara sauce.

Makes 4 wraps

AT-HOME COST: $7.50

TEXAS ROADHOUSE
legendary sirloin beef tips

TENDER PIECES OF SIRLOIN WITH SAUTÉED MUSHROOMS AND ONION IN A MADE-FROM-SCRATCH BROWN GRAVY, SERVED WITH SEASONED RICE OR MASHED POTATOES.

Salt and pepper
Garlic powder
2 tablespoons all-purpose flour
1 tablespoon olive oil
4 to 6 ounces sirloin steak, cut into large dice
1 small onion, diced

2 tablespoons butter
4 large mushrooms, sliced
¼ cup white wine
½ cup beef broth
1 tablespoon cornstarch
Seasoned rice or mashed potatoes, for serving

1. Mix salt and pepper and the garlic powder together and combine with the flour. Heat the oil in a skillet. Dredge the steak pieces with the flour mixture, then sauté the meat until it is medium-rare. Add the onion and cook until it is softened.

2. Add the butter to the pan and then add the mushrooms. Cook until the mushrooms begin to color, then remove the meat, onion, and mushrooms to a platter and keep warm.

3. Deglaze the skillet with the wine, making sure to loosen any browned bits, and let it reduce a little. Add the beef broth and bring to a boil, then return the reserved meat and vegetables to the pan and simmer, covered, for about 1 hour, or until the meat is tender.

4. Mix the cornstarch with a little of the cooking liquid to make a paste and add it to the simmering broth. When the sauce is thickened, serve the tips with rice, mashed potatoes, or a vegetable of your choice.

Serves 1

AT-HOME COST: $5

TEXAS ROADHOUSE
texas steak rolls

DEEP-FRIED EGG ROLLS STUFFED WITH SEASONED SIRLOIN, CHEESE, AND ONION, WITH A BIT OF HEAT FROM JALAPEÑOS, SERVED WITH A CREAMY BARBECUE DIPPING SAUCE.

Dipping Sauce
3 cups mayonnaise
1 cup barbecue sauce
1 tablespoon black pepper
1 tablespoon white pepper
1 tablespoon red pepper

Texas Rolls
2 pounds grilled or broiled sirloin steak, diced into ½-inch pieces

1 pound Cheddar cheese, shredded
½ cup onion, cut into ¼-inch dice
2 jalapeño peppers, minced
1½ cups barbecue sauce, homemade or store-bought
1 large egg, beaten
24 egg roll wrappers (7-inch square size)
3 cups vegetable oil, for frying

1. Do ahead: Make the dipping sauce by whisking all the sauce ingredients together. Refrigerate in a covered container until ready to use.

2. Combine the steak pieces, Cheddar cheese, onion, and jalapeños. Add the barbecue sauce and mix well.

3. Whisk together the egg and ½ cup water to make an egg wash.

4. Fill each wrapper with ⅓ cup of the meat mixture, following the procedure on page 274 or on the egg roll wrapper package. Seal the corners of the wrapper with the egg wash, pressing firmly to make sure they stick. Repeat with the remaining meat mixture and wrappers. Refrigerate for 30 minutes.

5. Heat the vegetable oil to 365°F in a wok or saucepan. Fry each roll until golden brown on all sides. Drain on paper towels and serve hot with the dipping sauce.

Serves 2 to 4

AT-HOME COST: $9.50

Substitute turkey or chicken for the steak and bake the egg rolls in a
375°F oven until browned.

T.G.I. FRIDAY'S
au gratin potatoes

CREAMY, CHEESY POTATOES BAKED TO PERFECTION.

4 large baking potatoes, scrubbed

Béchamel Sauce
5 tablespoons unsalted butter
¼ cup all-purpose flour
4 cups milk
2 teaspoons salt
¼ teaspoon ground nutmeg

1 teaspoon salt
¼ teaspoon white pepper
¾ cup grated mozzarella cheese
¼ cup grated Colby cheese

1. Do ahead: Bake the potatoes in a 400°F oven until tender, about 1 hour. Let cool long enough to be able to make neat slices, about 30 minutes, then slice into ½-inch-thick rounds.

2. To make the béchamel sauce, melt the butter in a saucepan and whisk in the flour, stirring constantly, until the paste is smooth and a very light brown. Gradually add the milk, whisking, and season with the 2 teaspoons salt and nutmeg. Lower the heat and simmer for 15 minutes, or until the sauce thickens.

3. Preheat the oven to 300°F.

4. Put the sliced potatoes in a large bowl and season with the 1 teaspoon salt and the white pepper. Add the mozzarella and Colby cheeses, then fold in 3 cups of the warm béchamel sauce. Transfer the mixture to a 13 by 9-inch baking dish and cover with foil.

5. Bake until the cheese melts, then remove the foil and let the top get bubbly and brown. Serve hot.

Serves 4

AT-HOME COST: $7.50

Leftover baked potatoes can be used in this recipe.

T.G.I. Friday's, one of the first American casual dining chains, is a dining experience that has become a favorite pastime of millions since 1965. The first T.G.I. Friday's was located at First Avenue and 63rd Street in New York City. The chain's focus is on providing a comfortable, relaxing environment where patrons can enjoy high-quality food and have a good time.

T.G.I. FRIDAY'S
bruschetta chicken

ANGEL HAIR PASTA IS TOSSED WITH A BRUSCHETTA MARINARA SAUCE, TOPPED WITH JUICY STRIPS OF BROILED CHICKEN BREAST AND SHAVINGS OF PARMESAN CHEESE, DRIZZLED WITH BALSAMIC GLAZE, AND SERVED WITH TOASTED GARLIC BREAD.

Balsamic Glaze
1 cup balsamic vinegar
1 tablespoon sugar

Garlic Butter
8 tablespoons (1 stick) butter, softened
½ teaspoon garlic powder
Salt and pepper

Marinated Tomatoes
5 fresh basil leaves, shredded
6 to 8 medium Roma tomatoes, diced
2 cloves garlic, minced
2 tablespoons olive oil

Bruschetta Marinara Sauce
2 cloves garlic, sliced
¼ cup olive oil
¼ teaspoon salt
⅛ teaspoon pepper
½ cup tomato sauce, homemade or store-bought
5 fresh basil leaves, shredded

1 loaf French or Italian bread

Chicken and Pasta
4 boneless, skinless chicken breasts
Salt and pepper
1 pound angel hair pasta, cooked according to the package directions
Parmesan cheese, shaved

1. Do ahead: Make the balsamic glaze in a small saucepan. Simmer the vinegar and sugar until it is reduced to ¼ cup.

2. Do ahead: For the garlic butter, combine the softened butter, garlic powder, and salt and pepper.

3. Do ahead: Make the marinated tomatoes: Add the shredded basil to the diced tomatoes and toss with the minced garlic and the 2 tablespoons olive oil. Set aside until needed.

4. To make the marinara sauce, sauté the garlic slices in the ¼ cup olive oil along with 2 tablespoons of the garlic butter until the garlic softens. Add

the salt, pepper, tomato sauce, and shredded basil. Simmer for about 5 minutes. Take the pan off the heat and set aside.

5. Preheat the broiler.

6. Split the loaf of bread lengthwise and spread with the remaining garlic butter. Toast the bread halves until the butter is melted and the bread is a light golden brown.

7. Season the chicken with salt and pepper and broil, turning once, until cooked through and no longer pink in the middle. Slice each breast into 4 strips.

8. Combine the marinated tomatoes with the marinara sauce. Toss the angel hair pasta with the mixture and divide among 4 plates. Layer the chicken strips over the pasta. Drop a few shavings of Parmesan on top and drizzle the whole serving with the balsamic glaze. Serve with the toasted garlic bread on the side.

Serves 4

AT-HOME COST: $9.50

The bruschetta marinara sauce makes a good dip as well as a topping for bruschetta.

T.G.I. FRIDAY'S
lemon chicken scaloppine

CHICKEN, MUSHROOMS, AND ARTICHOKE WITH A HINT OF CITRUS IN A CREAM-BASED CHABLIS SAUCE OVER PASTA.

Lemon Cream Sauce
1 cup Chablis or other medium-dry white wine
2 teaspoons lemon juice
1 tablespoon butter
1 cup heavy cream
½ teaspoon dried thyme
Salt and pepper

Chicken
¼ cup olive oil
1 boneless, skinless chicken breast, pounded ¼ inch thick
1 cup sliced mushrooms

Juice of 1 lemon
2 tablespoons heavy cream
½ canned artichoke, halved and split lengthwise
1 teaspoon minced fresh parsley

4 ounces angel hair pasta, cooked according to the package directions

Garnish
2 tablespoons pancetta, diced and fried
1 tablespoon drained capers

1. To make the lemon cream sauce, boil the wine and lemon juice until reduced to ¼ cup. Lower the heat and whisk in the butter. Add the cream and simmer until slightly thickened. Season with the dried thyme and salt and pepper, and set aside.

2. Heat the olive oil in a skillet and sauté the chicken breast, turning once, until it is cooked through and no longer pink in the middle. Add the sliced mushrooms and sauté until they absorb some of the liquid. Add the lemon juice and stir to blend. Add the 2 tablespoons cream and stir well.

3. Add the lemon cream sauce and the artichoke to the skillet, simmering for a few minutes. Add the parsley and stir.

4. Mound the cooked pasta into a warmed bowl and top with the chicken breast. Pour the mushroom–lemon cream sauce over the chicken and the pasta. Garnish with the diced pancetta and the capers.

Serves 1

AT-HOME COST: $7.00

Use regular bacon that has been diced and cooked rather than the pancetta, if you prefer.

T.G.I. FRIDAY'S
nine-layer dip

A LAYERED DIP OF REFRIED BEANS, SOUR CREAM, GUACAMOLE, TOMATOES, OLIVES, AND CHEESE SERVED WITH ASSORTED DIPPERS.

2 slices bacon, diced
One 16-ounce can refried beans
½ cup sour cream
½ teaspoon taco seasoning mix
¾ cup shredded Cheddar cheese
¾ cup guacamole, homemade or store-bought

½ cup diced tomatoes
1 tablespoon minced fresh cilantro
2 tablespoons sliced pitted black olives
2 tablespoons finely sliced green onions
Tortilla strips and assorted chips

1. Sauté the bacon in a skillet. Add the refried beans and blend well. Set aside.

2. Combine the sour cream with the taco seasoning. Set aside.

3. Build the dip in a shallow platter, layer by layer, in the following order:

   Bacon and beans, spread in a 1-inch-thick layer
   ¼ cup plus 2 tablespoons Cheddar cheese
   Sour cream mixture
   Guacamole
   Diced tomatoes
   Cilantro
   Black olives
   Green onions
   ¼ cup plus 2 tablespoons Cheddar cheese

4. Surround the layered dip with tortilla strips and assorted chips.

Serves 4 to 6

AT-HOME COST: $5

This layered dip can be made ahead and refrigerated, covered in plastic wrap, overnight. Just add the chips the next day and enjoy your party! Bring to room temperature before serving.

T.G.I. FRIDAY'S
spicy cajun chicken pasta

CAJUN-SPICED CHICKEN WITH A TOMATO AND PEPPER SAUCE SERVED OVER FETTUCCINE PASTA.

4 tablespoons (½ stick) butter
1 green bell pepper, chopped
1 red bell pepper, chopped
1 cup sliced onion
1 clove garlic, minced
2 boneless, skinless chicken breasts
2 teaspoons olive oil

Sauce
4 to 6 mushrooms, sliced
1 medium tomato, chopped
1 cup chicken broth
1½ teaspoons salt

¼ teaspoon cayenne pepper
¼ teaspoon paprika
¼ teaspoon white pepper
¼ teaspoon dried thyme

Pasta
12 ounces fettuccine pasta, cooked according to the package directions, with
1½ teaspoons salt
2 tablespoons butter
2 teaspoons chopped fresh parsley, for garnish

1. In a large skillet, melt the 4 tablespoons butter and sauté the bell peppers, onion, and garlic for about 8 minutes, or until the vegetables are soft. Set aside.

2. Cut the chicken into bite-size pieces and sauté in the olive oil until cooked through. Using a slotted spoon, transfer the chicken pieces to the pan with the sautéed vegetables.

3. To make the sauce, in the same pan you used to cook the chicken, sauté the mushrooms just a bit, until they absorb some of the liquid. Then add the tomato, chicken broth, salt, cayenne, paprika, white pepper, and thyme. Simmer for 10 minutes, until the sauce is slightly thickened.

4. Add the simmered sauce to the chicken and vegetables and simmer for another 5 minutes, until everything is heated through and the flavors are well combined.

5. Toss the pasta with the 2 tablespoons butter and plate individually. Top with the chicken and sauce, garnish with the parsley, and serve.

Serves 2 as an entrée or 4 as a side dish

AT-HOME COST: $9.50

THAI KITCHEN
fried rice (khau phat)

FRIED RICE WITH CHICKEN AND VEGETABLES, EGG, TOMATO, AND THAI CHILI
SAUCE.

2 tablespoons vegetable oil
1 clove garlic, minced
½ cup chopped onion
4 ounces boneless, skinless
chicken breast, sliced into thin
strips
½ cup assorted vegetables, such
as bell pepper strips, sliced
carrots, and snow peas

1 medium tomato, diced
2 cups jasmine rice, cooked
according to the package
directions and chilled
2 tablespoons spicy Thai chili
sauce
1 tablespoon fish sauce (nam pla)
1 egg, lightly beaten

1. Heat 1 tablespoon of the vegetable oil in a wok or large skillet and
   sauté the garlic and onion until soft and only slightly colored brown.
   Add the chicken strips and stir-fry for 2 minutes, then add the vegetables. Stir-fry for another 3 minutes, or until the chicken is cooked
   through.

2. Stir in the tomato, cooked rice, chili sauce, and fish sauce. Cook for
   3 minutes, or until the sauce begins to simmer.

3. Push the contents of the wok to one side and add the remaining
   1 tablespoon vegetable oil and the beaten egg. Scramble the egg until it
   is set, then mix it in with the rice mixture. Toss everything once to
   blend, and serve hot.

Serves 2

AT-HOME COST: $5

Use 4 ounces peeled and deveined small shrimp instead of the chicken.

THAI KITCHEN

sesame chicken

LIGHTLY COATED CHICKEN PIECES DEEP-FRIED UNTIL GOLDEN AND COATED WITH A SESAME SAUCE.

¼ cup sesame seeds

Sauce
½ cup water
½ cup vinegar
¼ teaspoon salt
1¾ cups sugar
1 tablespoon soy sauce
Yellow food coloring (optional)

Chicken
1 cup all-purpose flour
½ cup cornstarch
½ teaspoon salt
½ teaspoon pepper
4 cups thinly sliced chicken
   breast (about 1½ pounds)
2 cups vegetable oil, for frying

1. Do ahead: Toast the sesame seeds in a small dry skillet over medium heat just until they take on a little color and begin to release their aroma. Remove from the pan and set aside or store in a covered container until ready to use.

2. Do ahead: Make the sauce. Combine all the sauce ingredients in a large pot. Cook over medium-high heat until the sugar has caramelized, about 20 minutes. Do not allow the mixture to boil over. Remove from the heat; set aside.

3. In a small bowl, combine the flour, cornstarch, salt, and pepper. Dredge the chicken slices with the mixture.

4. In a wok or skillet, heat the vegetable oil to 350°F and add the chicken, working in batches. The coating of the chicken should be a light brown. Drain on paper towels.

5. To serve, toss the chicken in a large warmed bowl with the sauce and sesame seeds. Serve hot.

Serves 4

AT-HOME COST: $8.50

THAI KITCHEN BURBANK
tiger roast chicken

HALVED CHICKEN, MARINATED IN A SPECIAL SAUCE AND ROASTED UNTIL TENDER—TOPPED WITH FRESH LEMONGRASS.

⅓ cup Thai oyster sauce
6 cloves garlic, minced
1 teaspoon pepper
1 tablespoon Thai soy sauce or
   regular soy sauce

1 tablespoon sugar
1 teaspoon sea salt
¼ cup minced fresh lemongrass,
   plus extra for garnish
One 2-pound chicken, halved

1. Do ahead: Combine the oyster sauce, garlic, pepper, soy sauce, sugar, sea salt, and the ¼ cup lemongrass in a large bowl. Add the chicken halves and make sure they are well coated with the marinade. Cover and refrigerate overnight.

2. Preheat the oven to 375°F.

3. Remove the chicken from the marinade and place it in a roasting pan, skin side up. Discard the marinade. Roast for 35 to 45 minutes, until the juices run clear.

4. Garnish with additional lemongrass.

Serves 2

AT-HOME COST: $7

Substitute 1½ teaspoons grated lemon zest for the lemongrass.

 Thai oyster sauce, soy sauce, and sweet hot sauce are available at Thai markets.

TONY ROMA'S
baked potato soup

A GREAT WAY TO USE LEFTOVER BAKED POTATOES. TOPPED WITH SHREDDED CHEDDAR CHEESE, BACON, AND CHIVES.

3 tablespoons butter
1 cup diced onions
2 tablespoons all-purpose flour
4 cups chicken broth
¼ cup cornstarch
1½ cups instant potato flakes
1 teaspoon salt
¾ teaspoon pepper
½ teaspoon dried basil

Pinch of dried thyme
2 baked potatoes, peeled and
   chopped (about 2 cups)
1 cup half-and-half

Garnish
½ cup shredded Cheddar cheese
¼ cup crumbled cooked bacon
Snipped fresh chives

1. Melt the butter in a stockpot and sauté the onions until slightly browned. Whisk in the flour, stirring constantly until the paste is smooth. Gradually add the chicken broth and 2 cups of water. Bring the pot to a boil, then add the cornstarch and instant potato flakes. Season with the salt and pepper and add the dried herbs. Lower the heat and simmer for 5 minutes.

2. Add the chopped potatoes and the half-and-half, bring the pot back up to a boil, then reduce the heat and simmer for 15 minutes, or until thickened.

3. Ladle the soup into warmed bowls and garnish with the Cheddar cheese, crumbled bacon, and chives.

Serves 6 to 8

AT-HOME COST: $7

Bake the potatoes the day before.

The first Tony Roma's was opened in North Miami, Florida, in 1972. Known as the pioneer of baby back ribs, today Tony Roma's is a worldwide success with nearly two hundred restaurants in thirty-two countries.

UNO CHICAGO GRILL
classic deep-dish pizza

CRUMBLED SAUSAGE, CHUNKY TOMATO SAUCE, MOZZARELLA, AND GRATED ROMANO MAKE FOR A CLASSIC DEEP-DISH PIZZA.

Dough

1 envelope (2¼ teaspoons) active dry yeast

1 cup warm water (110° to 115°F)

3½ cups all-purpose flour, plus extra for dusting

½ cup coarsely ground cornmeal

1 teaspoon salt

¼ cup vegetable oil

Pizza Topping

1 pound Italian sausage, removed from the casings

One 15-ounce can whole tomatoes

1 pound mozzarella, thinly sliced

2 cloves garlic, minced

5 fresh basil leaves, finely chopped

¼ cup grated Romano cheese

Special Equipment

One 15-inch deep-dish pizza pan

1. In a large bowl, proof the yeast in the warm water until it foams, about 5 minutes. Add 1 cup of the flour, the cornmeal, salt, and vegetable oil. Stir to combine everything.

2. Continue adding the flour ½ cup at a time, stirring well after each addition, until the flour is used up. The dough should form a soft ball and come away from the sides of the bowl.

3. Flour a work surface and begin to knead the dough until it reaches elasticity and is no longer very sticky, 10 to 12 minutes. Put the ball of dough in a greased bowl, turning once to grease all sides, and cover with a damp dish towel. Set the bowl in an area free of drafts. Let the dough rise until doubled in size, about 1 hour.

4. Punch the dough down and briefly knead on a floured surface, about 2 minutes. Press the dough into a greased 15-inch deep-dish pizza pan until it comes up the 2-inch sides of the pan and is even on the bottom. Cover and let rise for about 20 minutes.

5. Prepare the topping: Sauté the sausage until it is cooked through, crumbling it as it cooks. Drain off the fat and set it aside. Drain the tomatoes and coarsely chop them.

6. Preheat the oven to 500°F.

7. When the dough has completed the second rising, layer the sliced mozzarella over the bottom of the dough, followed by the sausage and then the garlic. Finish with the chopped tomatoes and the basil, and sprinkle with the grated Romano cheese.

8. Bake for 15 minutes at 500°F, then turn down the oven temperature to 400°F and bake for another 25 to 35 minutes. One way to check the cooking time is to lift up a section of the crust and check the color. The crust should be a dark golden brown and be slightly crispy. When ready to serve, cut into slices and serve hot.

Serves 8

AT-HOME COST: $7.50

Change the flavor of your pizza by changing the herbs. Try dried oregano or marjoram, or combinations of several different kinds.

Uno Chicago Grill, formerly Pizzeria Uno, started as a Chicago-style pizza place in Chicago selling pasta and sandwiches as well. It was opened in 1943 by Ike Sewell.

WINGER'S
sticky fingers

WANT THE WINGS WITHOUT THE BONES? NOW YOU'VE GOT THE ANSWER.
WINGER'S STICKY FINGERS ARE MADE FROM TENDER, BONELESS CHICKEN
BREASTS, DRENCHED IN THEIR ORIGINAL AMAZING SAUCE.

Original Amazing Sauce
⅓ cup packed dark brown sugar
⅓ cup Worcestershire
   sauce
¼ cup ketchup
1 tablespoon honey

2 teaspoons Tabasco
2 teaspoons apple cider vinegar

One 12- to 16-ounce box frozen
   breaded chicken tenders
Nonstick cooking spray

1. Preheat the oven to 350°F.
2. In a small saucepan, combine all the sauce ingredients and simmer until warmed through.
3. Bake the chicken tenders according to the package directions.
4. Spray a baking sheet with cooking spray. Toss the cooked chicken in the sauce, then remove each piece to the prepared baking sheet.
5. Bake for 5 to 8 minutes—the sauce should thicken and become sticky. Remove the chicken from the oven and let sit for a minute or two to allow the sauce to firm up a little.
6. Serve the sticky fingers with the remaining sauce for dipping.

Serves 2 to 4

AT-HOME COST: $6

Of course, this makes a great sauce for chicken wings as well.

In 1993, The Slaymaker Group opened the first Winger's—
An American Diner. Their concept was to create a cost-effective yet
distinctive restaurant with exceptional menu items. Today they have
more than forty franchise locations in eight states with plans to
expand throughout the United States.

ZINFANDEL RESTAURANT
barbecued ribs

BARBECUED RIBS SEASONED WITH THEIR SIGNATURE RIB RUB AND SLATHERED WITH THEIR SIGNATURE TANGY BARBECUE SAUCE.

Zinfandel Rib Rub
1 tablespoon kosher salt
1 tablespoon granulated sugar
1 tablespoon packed dark brown sugar
1 tablespoon chile powder (not chili powder, which is a blend of seasonings)

1 tablespoon ground cumin
1 tablespoon pepper
2 tablespoons paprika

½ slab pork spareribs (about 1 pound)
½ cup Zinfandel Barbecue Sauce (page 301)

1. Do ahead: Make the rib rub by thoroughly combining all the ingredients. The rub can be stored in a covered container until ready to use. Makes ½ cup.

2. Do ahead: Put the slab of ribs on a baking sheet and sprinkle with the rib rub. Start massaging the mixture into both sides of the meat. Any rub that falls onto the baking sheet should be scooped up and reapplied to the ribs. Cover in plastic wrap and refrigerate for at least 4 hours before you start the grill, or, if possible, overnight.

3. Preheat the grill.

4. Grill the ribs, bone side down, for 30 minutes, covered, then turn them skin side down and grill for an additional 30 minutes, covered. The meat should be falling off the bones and crispy around the edges. Serve with the barbecue sauce.

Serves 1

AT-HOME COST: $9.75

Removing the silver skin before massaging the rub on the slab will make these ribs extra tender and melt-in-your-mouth fantastic!

The ribs can be chilled immediately after grilling and reheated on the grill to save time.

Zinfandel Restaurant was an independent restaurant in Chicago owned by Susan and Drew Goss that specialized in ethnic American cooking. In recent years, the couple has closed Zinfandel and opened the West Town Tavern, which is also in Chicago. Restaurateurs for the past twenty years, the Gosses have received accolades from *The Wine Spectator* (Awards of Excellence from 1993 to 2001), *Chicago* magazine (one of the Best New Restaurants 1994, top Chicago restaurants 1997, 1999), *Esquire,* and *Gourmet.* Zinfandel received the coveted DiRona Award for 1999, 2000, 2001, and 2002.

ZINFANDEL
RESTAURANT
barbecue sauce

ZINFANDEL'S SIGNATURE TANGY BARBECUE SAUCE.

1½ cups finely chopped red onions
1 tablespoon corn oil
3 cups canned tomatoes, diced, with juice
2 tablespoons cider vinegar
1½ teaspoons kosher salt
¾ teaspoon pepper
¼ teaspoon dried thyme
Pinch of ground cumin

1½ tablespoons paprika
1 teaspoon chile powder (not chili powder, which is a blend of seasonings)
½ teaspoon dried oregano
1½ tablespoons Worcestershire sauce
¼ cup dark molasses
½ cup orange juice

1. Sauté the onions in the corn oil until translucent. Add the remaining ingredients except for the orange juice and simmer for 10 minutes over low heat, stirring frequently. Let cool.

2. Add the orange juice to the cooled mixture and puree in a blender. This recipe makes about 4 cups of sauce, so refrigerate what you don't need for the ribs in a covered container. This can also be divided among smaller containers and individually frozen.

Makes about 4 cups

AT-HOME COST: $5

ZINFANDEL RESTAURANT
crusty duckling hash

CHUNKS OF ROASTED DUCKLING MIXED WITH BELL PEPPERS, POTATOES, AND ZINFANDEL'S OWN BARBECUE SAUCE, SHAPED INTO PATTIES AND SEARED ON A HOT GRIDDLE. DELICIOUS WITH A CRISP GREEN SALAD!

Roasted Vegetables

2 cups small red potatoes, scrubbed and quartered

½ cup thinly sliced red onion

¼ cup thinly sliced red bell pepper

¼ cup thinly sliced yellow bell pepper

2 cloves garlic, minced

2 tablespoons olive oil

2 cups diced roasted duck meat

2 tablespoons tomato-based barbecue sauce, such as Zinfandel Barbecue Sauce (page 301)

1 tablespoon Worcestershire sauce

1 tablespoon shredded basil leaves

½ teaspoon kosher salt

½ teaspoon pepper

1½ cups mashed potatoes

1½ teaspoons chile powder (not chili powder, which is a blend of seasonings)

2 tablespoons olive oil

1. Do ahead: Roast the vegetables. Preheat the oven to 400°F. In a large bowl, mix the red potatoes, onion, bell peppers, and garlic with the 2 tablespoons olive oil. Spread out the vegetables on a baking sheet and roast for about 20 minutes.

2. In a large bowl, mix the diced duck meat with the roasted vegetables and add the barbecue sauce, Worcestershire sauce, basil, salt, and pepper. Mix well to make sure all the ingredients are well distributed. Add the mashed potatoes and the chile powder, taste for seasonings, and mix one more time.

3. Shape the mixture into 6 equal portions and make round patties, as you would for hamburgers. If you have pastry rings, choose one of the larger rings and use this as a form for the patties. Refrigerate the patties for at least 1 hour.

4. Heat the olive oil in a large skillet and let it get almost smoking hot. Add the patties and let them sit until a brown crust forms on the bottom (moving them around will disturb the mix and they could crumble). When a solid crust has formed on the bottom, turn each one over, carefully, and lower the heat. Let them get brown on the underside. The centers should be heated through.

Makes 6 patties

AT-HOME COST: $5

Substitute cooked, diced chicken or turkey for the duckling.

Once the mixture has been thoroughly combined, it may be covered and refrigerated until needed.

ZINFANDEL RESTAURANT

watercress, walnut, and blue cheese salad

A SIMPLE WATERCRESS SALAD WITH A HINT OF BLUE CHEESE AND THE CRUNCH OF TOASTED WALNUTS IN A LIGHT VINAIGRETTE DRESSING.

½ cup chopped walnuts, toasted
2 tablespoons lemon juice
3 tablespoons olive oil
Salt and pepper

3 cups watercress, trimmed and washed
½ cup crumbled blue cheese

1. Do ahead: Toast the walnuts in a small skillet over medium heat until they just begin to color, about 5 minutes. Stir frequently, so they do not burn. Let cool and set aside until ready to use, or store in a covered container.

2. Combine the lemon juice and the olive oil in a large bowl and whisk to blend. Season with a little salt and pepper. Toss with the watercress.

3. Plate the salad and garnish with the blue cheese and toasted walnuts.

Serves 3

AT-HOME COST: $4.50

 Substitute feta cheese for the blue cheese if you prefer something lighter.

ZINFANDEL RESTAURANT

tortilla soup

ALL YOUR FAVORITE SOUTHWESTERN FLAVORS: TORTILLAS, CILANTRO, AND A LITTLE CAYENNE.

4 large onions, or enough for
  2 cups onion puree
1½ teaspoons chopped garlic
8 corn tortillas, coarsely
  chopped
2 teaspoons vegetable oil
1 teaspoon cayenne pepper
2 teaspoons ground cumin
3 bay leaves
¾ cup tomato paste
1½ teaspoons chicken bouillon
  powder

¼ cup chopped fresh cilantro
2 teaspoons chopped fresh
  epazote
Salt and white pepper
2 cooked chicken breasts, diced

Garnish
1 avocado, pitted, peeled, and
  chopped
Shredded Monterey Jack cheese
1 corn tortilla, cut into thin strips
  and fried

1. Do ahead: Make the onion puree: Peel and chop the 4 large onions. Add ¼ cup of water and microwave or simmer in a saucepan until they are just softened. Puree in a blender until smooth, then strain out the liquid using a fine-mesh strainer. Set aside or refrigerate, covered, until ready to use.

2. Sauté the garlic and chopped tortillas in the vegetable oil in a stockpot until softened. Add the strained onion puree, the cayenne, cumin, bay leaves, tomato paste, bouillon powder, and ½ cup of water. Simmer for about 20 minutes, or until the tortillas have completely fallen apart. Add the cilantro and epazote, and remove the bay leaves.

3. Transfer the soup in batches to a food processor and pulse until just blended. You can also use a blender to process until just blended. Taste for seasonings and add salt and white pepper.

4. Ladle the soup into warmed bowls and add the diced chicken, chopped avocado, shredded Monterey Jack, and fried tortilla strips. You can freeze half this soup for later, before adding the fresh garnishes.

Serves 8

AT-HOME COST: $7

Epazote is an herb used as a leafy vegetable in Mexican cooking. Substitute celery leaves if you can't find the epazote.

Buy some multicolored tortilla chips to crumble and use as a garnish.

MEASUREMENTS

Pinch or dash	Less than ⅛ teaspoon
3 teaspoons	1 tablespoon
4 tablespoons	¼ cup
8 tablespoons	½ cup
12 tablespoons	¾ cup
16 tablespoons	1 cup
2 cups	1 pint
4 cups	1 quart
4 quarts	1 gallon
8 tablespoons butter	1 stick butter
4 sticks butter	1 pound butter
16 ounces	1 pound
1 fluid ounce	2 tablespoons
8 fluid ounces	1 cup
16 fluid ounces	1 pint
32 fluid ounces	1 quart

Use standard measuring cups and spoons. All measurements are level.

TRADEMARKS

- A&W is a registered trademark of Yum! Brands, Inc.
- Applebee's is a registered trademark of Applebee's International, Inc.
- Aunt Chilada's is a registered trademark of Grupo Aunt Chilada's, LLC.
- Bahama Breeze is a registered trademark of Darden Concepts, Inc.
- Benihana is a registered trademark of Benihana, Inc.
- Bravo! Cucina Italiana is a registered trademark of BRAVO | BRIO Restaurant Group, Inc.
- Buca di Beppo is a registered trademark of Planet Hollywood International, Inc.
- California Pizza Kitchen is a registered trademark of California Pizza Kitchen, Inc.
- Carrabba's is a registered trademark of OSI Restaurant Partners, LLC.
- The Cheesecake Factory is a registered trademark of The Cheesecake Factory, Inc.
- Chevys Fresh Mex is a registered trademark of Real Mex Restaurants, Inc.
- Chi-Chi's is a registered trademark of Chi-Chi's, Inc., and Prandium, Inc.
- Chili's is a registered trademark of Brinker International.
- Chipotle Mexican Grill is a registered trademark of Chipotle Mexican Grill, Inc.
- Claim Jumper is a registered trademark of Claim Jumper Restaurants, LLC.
- Dave and Buster's is a registered trademark of Dave & Buster's, Inc.
- Don Pablo's is a registered trademark of Rita Restaurant Corp.
- Emeril's New Orleans Restaurant is a registered trademark of Food of Love Productions, LLC.
- Famous Dave's is a registered trademark of Famous Dave's of America, Inc.

- Garibaldi Cafe is a registered trademark of Garibaldi Management Corporation.
- Golden Corral is a registered trademark of the Golden Corral Corporation.
- Hard Rock Cafe is a registered trademark of Hard Rock America, Inc.
- Houston's is a registered trademark of Hillstone Restaurant Group.
- Jack in the Box is a registered trademark of Jack in the Box, Inc.
- Joe's Crab Shack is a registered trademark of Landry's Seafood Restaurants, Inc.
- KFC is a registered trademark of Yum! Brands, Inc.
- Luby's Cafeteria is a registered trademark of Luby's, Inc.
- Macaroni Grill is a registered trademark of Brinker International.
- Mrs. Fields is a registered trademark of Mrs. Fields Original Cookies, Inc.
- O'Charley's is a registered trademark of O'Charley's Inc.
- The Old Spaghetti Factory is a registered trademark of The Dussin Group.
- Olive Garden is a registered trademark of Darden Restaurants, Inc.
- Outback Steakhouse is a registered trademark of Outback Steakhouse, Inc.
- Panda Express is a registered trademark of Panda Restaurant Group, Inc.
- Panera Bread is a registered trademark of Panera Bread.
- Pepperidge Farm is a registered trademark of Campbell Soup Company.
- P.F. Chang's China Bistro is a registered trademark of P.F. Chang's China Bistro, Inc.
- Ponderosa Steakhouse is a registered trademark of Homestyle Dining, LLC.
- Radisson Inn is a registered trademark of Carlson Hotels Worldwide, Inc.
- Red Lobster is a registered trademark of Darden Restaurants, Inc.
- Red Robin Gourmet Burgers, Inc.
- Ruby Tuesday is a registered trademark of Morrison Restaurants, Inc.
- Ruth's Chris Steak House is a registered trademark of Ruth's Hospitality Group, Inc.

- Sara Lee is a registered trademark of Sara Lee Corporation.
- Sbarro is a registered trademark of Sbarro, Inc.
- Shoney's is a registered trademark of Shoney's, Inc.
- Sonic Drive-In is a registered trademark of Sonic Corp.
- Starbucks is a registered trademark of Starbucks Corporation.
- Steak and Ale is a registered trademark of Atalaya Capital Management.
- Texas Roadhouse is a registered trademark of Texas Roadhouse, Inc.
- T.G.I. Friday's is a registered trademark of T.G.I. Friday's, Inc.
- Thai Kitchen is a registered trademark of Simply Asia Foods, Inc.
- Tony Roma's is a registered trademark of Tony Roma's, Inc.
- Uno Chicago Grill is a registered trademark of Pizzeria Uno Corporation.
- Winger's is a registered trademark of Winger's Grill and Bar.
- Zinfandel Restaurant is a registered trademark of West Town Tavern.

RESTAURANT WEBSITES

To find a restaurant near you, please visit:

A&W	www.awrestaurants.com
Applebee's	www.applebees.com
Aunt Chilada's	www.auntchiladas.com
Bahama Breeze	www.bahamabreeze.com
Benihana	www.benihana.com
Bravo! Cucina Italiana	www.bravoitalian.com
Buca di Beppo	www.bucadibeppo.com
California Pizza Kitchen	www.cpk.com
Carrabba's Italian Grill	www.carrabbas.com
The Cheesecake Factory	www.thecheesecakefactory.com
Chevys Fresh Mex	www.chevys.com
Chi-Chi's	www.chichis.com
Chili's	www.chilis.com
Chipotle Mexican Grill	www.chipotle.com
Claim Jumper	www.claimjumper.com
Dave and Buster's	www.daveandbusters.com
Don Pablo's	www.donpablos.com
Emeril's New Orleans Restaurant	www.emerils.com
Famous Dave's	www.famousdaves.com
Garibaldi Cafe	www.garibaldico.com
Golden Corral	www.goldencorral.com
Hard Rock Cafe	www.hardrock.com
Houston's	www.hillstone.com
Jack in the Box	www.jackinthebox.com
Joe's Crab Shack	www.joescrabshack.com
KFC	www.kfc.com
Luby's Cafeteria	www.lubys.com
Macaroni Grill	www.macaronigrill.com

Mrs. Fields	www.mrsfields.com
O'Charley's	www.ocharleys.com
The Old Spaghetti Factory	www.osf.com
Olive Garden	www.olivegarden.com
Outback Steakhouse	www.outback.com
Panda Express	www.pandaexpress.com
Panera Bread	www.panerabread.com
Pepperidge Farm	www.pepperidgefarm.com
P.F. Chang's China Bistro	www.pfchangs.com
Ponderosa Steakhouse	www.ponderosasteakhouses.com
Radisson Inn	www.radisson.com
Red Lobster	www.redlobster.com
Red Robin Gourmet Burgers	www.redrobin.com
Ruby Tuesday	www.rubytuesday.com
Ruth's Chris Steak House	www.ruthschris.com
Sara Lee	www.saralee.com
Sbarro	www.sbarro.com
Shoney's	www.shoneys.com
Sonic Drive-In	www.sonicdrivein.com
Starbucks	www.starbucks.com
Texas Roadhouse	www.texasroadhouse.com
T.G.I. Friday's	www.fridays.com
Thai Kitchen	www.thaikitchen.com
Thai Kitchen Burbank	www.thaikitchenburbank.com
Tony Roma's	www.tonyromas.com
Uno Chicago Grill	www.unos.com
Winger's	www.wingers.info
Zinfandel Restaurant	www.westtowntavern.com

INDEX